GCSE Science for AQA

AQA

Homework and Summary Book

**for AQA GCSE A & B, Additional
and Separate Sciences**

Gurinder Chadha
Katrina Fox
Lesley Owen

William Collins' dream of knowledge for all began with the publication of his first book in 1819. A self-educated mill worker, he not only enriched millions of lives, but also founded a flourishing publishing house. Today, staying true to this spirit, Collins books are packed with inspiration, innovation and practical expertise. They place you at the centre of a world of possibility and give you exactly what you need to explore it.

Collins. Freedom to teach.

Published by Collins
An imprint of HarperCollins*Publishers*
77–85 Fulham Palace Road
Hammersmith
London
W6 8JB

Browse the complete Collins catalogue at
www.collinseducation.com

© HarperCollins*Publishers* Limited 2006

10 9 8 7 6 5 4 3 2 1

ISBN-13 978 0 00 721633 8
ISBN-10 0 00 721633 5

British Library Cataloguing in Publication Data.
A Catalogue record for this publication is available from the British Library.

Commissioned by Cassandra Birmingham

Publishing Manager Michael Cotter

Project managed by Nicola Tidman

Edited by Lynn Watkins

Proofread by Ros Woodward

Cover artwork by Bob Lea

Cover design by Starfish

Internal design and page make-up by JPD

Illustrations by JPD, Peter Harper, Mark Walker, IFADesign Ltd and Peters and Zabransky

Production by Natasha Buckland

Printed and bound by the Bath Press, Glasgow and Bath

Acknowledgements
The Publishers gratefully acknowledge the following for permission to reproduce photographs. Whilst every effort has been made to trace the copyright holders, in cases where this has been unsuccessful or if any have been inadvertently overlooked, the Publishers will be pleased to make the necessary arrangements at the first opportunity.

p8 Alfred Pasieka / Science Photo Library; p10 © 2006 JupiterImages Corporation; p11 Michael W. Tweedie / Science Photo Library; p12 Simon Fraser / Science Photo Library; p13 Juz / Science Photo Library; p15 istockphoto; p17 istockphoto; p19 istockphoto; p21 istockphoto; p23 istockphoto, Andrew Lambert Photography / Science Photo Library; p25 istockphoto; p28 istockphoto; p30 istockphoto, © 2006 JupiterImages Corporation; p41 Chemical Design Ltd / Science Photo Library; p42 John Durham / Science Photo Library; p43 istockphoto; p45 Curt Maas / Agstock / Science Photo Library; p47 Bill Longcore / Science Photo Library; p48 BSIP, Veronique Estiot / Science Photo Library; p50 Francis Leroy, Biocosmos / Science Photo Library; p51 Simon Fraser / RVI, Newcastle-Upon-Tyne / Science Photo Library; p63 istockphoto; p64 istockphoto; p67 istockphoto, istockphoto; p70 istockphoto; p71 istockphoto; p75 istockphoto; p77 istockphoto; p78 Eye of Science / Science Photo Library; P79 Andrew Syred / Science Photo Library; p80 Alfred Pasieka / Science Photo Library; p81 Eye of Science / Science Photo Library; p82 Francis Leroy, Biocosmos / Science Photo Library; p83 National Cancer Institute / Science Photo Library; p85 Microfield Scientific Ltd / Science Photo Library; p86 John Bavosi / Science Photo Library; p87 AJ Photo / HOP Americain / Science Photo Library; p88 Brian Bell / Science Photo Library; p95 istockphoto; p99 istockphoto; p101 istockphoto; p103 istockphoto

Contents

Introduction   5

Biology B1a and B1b   6

Chemistry C1a and C1b   16

Physics P1a and P1b   28

Additional Biology   42

Additional Chemistry   54

Additional Physics   66

GCSE Biology   80

GCSE Chemistry   92

GCSE Physics   102

Exam-style questions   108

Model answers   116

Answers   124

Introduction

Welcome to Collins GCSE Science!

This Homework and Summary book is designed to help you get the most out of your GCSE Science studies. It covers GCSE Science, GCSE Additional Science, and GCSE Biology, Chemistry, Physics, all in one handy book!

There are several sections within the book. Here's how they work.

Summary content and Now Try This

This book is structured into topics which summarise the content you will learn on your course. The panels of summary points break all of the content down into short handy chunks to help you remember the key ideas. For more details, references to the relevant Collins Science textbook are also provided.

Within each summary panel there is a Now Try This box with practice questions. These questions are provided to help you check your own progress and understanding. Answers are provided at the back of the book.

At the top right of each page you will notice three circles. These are for you to mark in how well you feel you have understood everything on that page. For example:

 I have started this section but I don't completely understand or remember it all yet.

 I am getting better, but I have not yet been able to complete the Now Try This exercises correctly.

 I completely understand this section, and can complete all of the Now Try This exercises correctly.

Homework questions

Homework questions are provided for every topic. Your teacher will suggest which homework you should do.

Exam practice

The Exam-style questions pages will let you really prove you understand the Science, and will help you get ready for the exams. Note that these sample exam questions may cover content from more than one topic. This will help keep the key ideas you have learned fresh in your mind.

Model exam question answers

The Model answers are provided so you can see how questions should be answered.

We hope you find this Homework and Summary book useful. Good luck with your studies!

Your name _____

Class _____

In control

THE NERVOUS SYSTEM

- The **central nervous system (CNS)** is made up of the brain and spinal cord.
- **Receptors** in the sense organs detect **stimuli** (changes in the environment).
- **Sensory neurones** carry nerve impulses from receptors to the CNS.
- **Motor neurones** carry impulses from the CNS to **effectors** (muscles or glands).
- Tiny gaps called **synapses** are found where two neurones meet.
- A **reflex action** is a fast, automatic response to a stimulus.

 TOP TIP Nervous information passes along a neurone as an electrical impulse, but across a synapse as a chemical signal.

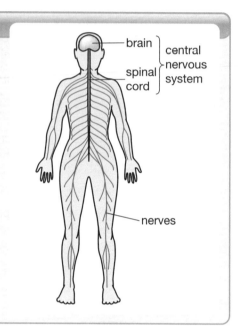
brain ⎫
spinal cord ⎬ central nervous system
⎭
nerves

Homework

1 List the **five** senses and state a) the organs involved and b) the receptors they contain.
2 Draw a flow diagram to show how the 'touching a hot object' reflex happens.
3 Describe and explain the different pathways of a reflex action and a conscious action.

HORMONES

- Keeping conditions inside the body constant is called **homeostasis**.
- **Hormones** are chemical messengers that control and coordinate processes within the body.
- They are secreted by **endocrine glands**.
- They are transported by the bloodstream to their **target organs**.
- Hormones act more slowly than the nervous system and their effects last longer.
- Hormones control things that require constant regulation, such as the levels of sugar and water in the blood, and the menstrual cycle in women.

Now Try This

a Complete the passage by filling in the missing words.

Hormones are _____ messengers that are _____ by endocrine _____. They travel in the _____ to their _____ organs where they have an effect. Hormonal control is often _____ than nervous control and its effects tend to be _____ lasting. Hormones control the levels of _____ and _____ in the blood.

Homework

4 List **three** human glands, the hormones they make and their target organs.
5 Sketch a diagram of the human body, labelling the positions of the following glands: pituitary, pancreas, adrenals, ovaries, testes.
6 State **three** differences between hormonal control and nervous control.

FERTILITY

- The **menstrual cycle** in women is controlled by the hormones **FSH**, **LH** and **oestrogen**.
- FSH and LH are secreted by the **pituitary gland**.
- FSH:
  - causes eggs to mature in the **ovaries**.
  - stimulates the ovaries to produce oestrogen.
- Oestrogen:
  - inhibits further production of FSH.
  - causes the uterus lining to thicken in preparation for pregnancy.
  - stimulates the pituitary gland to secrete LH.
- LH causes a mature egg to be released from an ovary (**ovulation**).

 TOP TIP The menstrual cycle lasts for an average of 28 days. Menstruation begins on day 1 and ovulation occurs at around day 14.

Now Try This

b Write FSH, LH or O (for oestrogen) to answer the following questions.

Which hormone inhibits the production of FSH by the pituitary gland? _____

Which hormone causes the lining of the uterus to thicken? _____

The ovaries are stimulated to produce oestrogen by which hormone? _____

Which hormone causes ovulation to occur? _____

Which hormone is produced by the ovaries? _____

Homework

7 Explain why oestrogen, used in the oral contraceptive pill, can be used to reduce fertility.

8 Research and write a paragraph on the advantages and disadvantages of the widespread use of oral contraceptives.

9 Explain why FSH can be used to treat infertility.

DRUGS, ALCOHOL AND TOBACCO

- A **drug** is a chemical that changes the processes in the body.
- Drugs such as **antibiotics** and **painkillers**, can be used to treat medical problems.
- Recreational drugs are used by choice because they make people feel different.
- If a person is **addicted** to a drug they may suffer **withdrawal symptoms** if they stop taking it.
- **Alcohol** can cause slower reactions, loss of self control, unconsciousness and coma. It can damage the brain and liver.
- Tobacco contains several harmful chemicals: **tar** causes cancer, **nicotine** is addictive and **carbon monoxide** reduces the amount of oxygen the blood can carry.
- Smoking tobacco can cause bronchitis, emphysema and lung cancer.

Now Try This

c What do you know about smoking? True (T) or false (F):

Most people take up smoking when they are adults. _____

Pregnant women who smoke have smaller babies. _____

Low-tar cigarettes do not cause lung cancer. _____

Giving up smoking will not reduce the risk of dying from cancer. _____

Smoking relieves stress and so helps to lower blood pressure. _____

You can die from lung cancer even if you don't smoke. _____

Homework

10 Write a paragraph about why driving under the influence of drugs and alcohol is illegal.

11 Make a list of any legal drugs you can think of and explain how/why they are used.

12 Explain how smoking causes emphysema.

Keeping healthy

HEALTHY DIET

- A **balanced diet** contains the correct amounts of **carbohydrates**, **fats**, **proteins**, **vitamins** and **minerals**, **fibre** and **water**.
- **Malnutrition** may lead to deficiency diseases and reduced resistance to infection.
- Lack of exercise and eating too much can lead to **obesity**.
- Too much salt in the diet can lead to high blood pressure (hypertension).
- **Cholesterol** is carried around in the blood as LDL or HDL cholesterol.
- Too much LDL cholesterol can cause heart disease.
- **Saturated fats** increase blood cholesterol levels, contributing to heart disease.

 It is the amount of saturated fats eaten, rather than cholesterol, that increases blood cholesterol levels.

Now Try This

a What do you know about eating a healthy diet? Are the following statements true (T) or false (F)?

Heart disease is caused entirely by genetic factors. _____

Cholesterol is an essential component of the diet. _____

Saturated fats are better for you than unsaturated fats. _____

Eating salt can help lower your blood pressure. _____

You do not need to exercise if you are thin. _____

Homework

1 Use the Internet to find out the recommended daily salt intake. Look at some food packets at home and find out the amount of salt they contain.
2 Give **three** examples of food containing **a)** saturated fats and **b)** unsaturated fats.
3 Write a paragraph to explain the effects of obesity on a person's health.

BACTERIA AND VIRUSES

- **Bacteria** and **viruses** are **microorganisms**, which reproduce very quickly.
- Bacteria are made of a single cell which is smaller than human cells.
- They can produce **toxins** (poisons) which can make us feel ill.
- Some bacteria are harmless and can actually be useful.
- Viruses are even smaller than bacteria and are not cells.
- Viruses 'hijack' our body's cells and reproduce inside them.
- Viruses burst out of the cells in which they reproduce, killing them.
- Bacteria and viruses that cause disease are called **pathogens**.

Now Try This

b Circle the correct answer.

Bacteria are smaller than:
    human cells   viruses   atoms

Viruses only grow in:
    food   cells   dirty conditions

Bacteria and viruses that cause disease are called:
    microorganisms   pathogens   germs

How many times smaller than bacteria are viruses?
    10   100   about 1000

Homework

4 List **three** examples of diseases caused by **a)** bacteria and **b)** viruses.
5 List **five** everyday measures you take to avoid being infected by bacteria and viruses.
6 Use the Internet to find **three** uses of bacteria.

BODY DEFENCES

- The **immune system** attacks and destroys **pathogens** that get inside the body.
- There are two types of **white blood cell**: **phagocytes** and **lymphocytes**.
- Phagocytes ingest ('eat') and digest pathogens to destroy them.

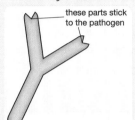

these parts stick to the pathogen

- Lymphocytes produce molecules called **antibodies**, which work against pathogens.
- Antibodies stick to pathogens and disable them so they can be easily attacked by phagocytes.
- **Antibiotics** are drugs that can help treat bacterial infections.

- The shape of a particular antibody means it can only stick to one kind of pathogen, a bit like how a key can only fit one lock.

Now Try This

c Match the following words to their descriptions.

i Bacteria or viruses which cause disease. — phagocytes

ii A molecule produced by lymphocytes. — antibiotic

iii A drug which can be used to treat bacterial infections. — antibody

iv White blood cells that produce antibodies against pathogens. — pathogens

v White blood cells that ingest and destroy pathogens. — lymphocytes

Homework

7 List **five** ways in which microorganisms can enter your body.

8 Why will your doctor not prescribe antibiotics for a cold or the flu?

9 In your own words, explain how white blood cells fight infection.

VACCINATION

- **Pathogens** have **antigens** on their surface which **antibodies** stick to.
- An antibody will only stick to one kind of antigen.
- When you are infected, the **lymphocytes** take time to make enough antibodies.
- If you are infected again, the lymphocytes 'remember' the antigen from last time.
- Antibodies are made so quickly that the infection is cleared before you get ill.
- **Vaccines** contain small amounts of dead or disabled pathogen that look the same as the 'real' pathogen but cannot make you ill.
- If you are infected afterwards by the 'real' pathogen, your lymphocytes are ready to make the correct antibody straight away, before you become ill.

TOP TIP Antigens and antibodies have very specific shapes and fit together like a key in a lock.

Now Try This

d Complete the passage by filling in the missing words.

There are two types of white blood cells. Phagocytes _____ ('eat') pathogens and _____ them. Lymphocytes produce molecules called _____ which stick to _____ on the surface of pathogens. After an infection, lymphocytes remember the antigen so if you are infected again antibodies are produced _____ before you get any _____.

Homework

10 Explain the difference between an antigen and an antibody.

11 Explain why you can only catch chicken pox once.

12 Use the Internet to find out about the risks and benefits of the MMR vaccine.

Reproduction and genes

REPRODUCTION

- Individuals need to reproduce to prevent a species from dying out.
- There are two types of **reproduction**: **sexual** and **asexual**.
- Asexual reproduction requires only one parent and produces genetically identical offspring (**clones**).
- Asexual reproduction allows organisms to reproduce very quickly, for example bacteria.
- Sexual reproduction requires two parents.
- **Gametes** (sex cells) from each parent join together (fuse) at **fertilisation**.
- Offspring contain genes from each parent and so show more **variation**.

 TOP TIP Individuals produced by asexual reproduction may show differences due to environmental factors.

Now Try This

a Complete the passage by filling in the missing words.

_____ reproduction needs just one parent. The offspring are genetically _____ to each other and to the _____. In _____ reproduction, two parents are needed, each producing _____ that join together during _____. The _____ have a mixture of the parents' genetic information and show more _____ than offspring produced asexually.

Homework

1 Draw a table to compare the features of sexual and asexual reproduction.
2 Use a search engine to find **five** examples of species which reproduce asexually.
3 Two strawberry plants are clones. Why might one be much bigger than the other?

YOU AND YOUR GENES

- Genetic information is found in the **nucleus** of a cell.
- **Chromosomes** are made up of the chemical **DNA** (deoxyribonucleic acid).
- A **gene** is a section of DNA that 'codes' for a **characteristic**, such as eye colour.
- Human body cells contain 23 pairs of chromosomes (46 in total).
- **Sperm** and **egg cells** each contain a set of 23 individual chromosomes.
- At fertilisation, the two sets of chromosomes combine to give an **embryo** with half of its genes coming from the mother and half from the father.

Now Try This

b Match the following words to their descriptions.

i The fusion (joining) of two gametes.	nucleus
ii A sex cell, such as a sperm or an egg.	chromosomes
iii Chemical from which chromosomes are made.	fertilisation
iv Part of the cell where chromosomes are found.	DNA
v Structures that contain genes and are found in the nucleus.	gamete

Homework

4 Explain how fertilisation in humans produces an embryo with 46 chromosomes.
5 Draw a diagram of a human cell, labelling the nucleus, chromosomes and a gene.
6 Make a list of characteristics that are completely determined by your genes.

GENETIC ENGINEERING

- **Genetic engineering** involves removing **genes** from one species and transferring them into another.
- For example, bacteria have been genetically engineered to produce human **insulin**.
- The insulin gene is first identified and removed from human cells.
- **Restriction enzymes** act like chemical 'scissors' to snip the wanted gene from the rest of the **chromosome**.
- This gene is then attached to chromosomes taken from bacteria.
- The modified chromosomes are put back into the bacteria, which now produce human insulin.
- Genes for **resistance** to pests and weedkillers can be transferred into plant cells by genetic engineering.

 TOP TIP Most diabetics use insulin produced by genetically engineered bacteria. It is cheaper and more effective than animal insulin.

Now Try This

c Put these sentences in the correct order.

☐ Put chromosomes back into bacteria.

☐ Choose the human gene required.

☐ Grow bacteria with the new gene to make insulin.

☐ Attach human gene to bacterial chromosome.

☐ Use restriction enzymes to remove the wanted gene.

Homework

7 Write a paragraph to explain your views on genetic engineering.

8 Use food labels to make a list of **five** items that contain GM ingredients.

9 Use the Internet to find **two** examples of genetic engineering.

CLONING

- **Clones** are genetically identical individuals.
- Producing new plants by taking **cuttings** from older plants is an example of cloning.
- **Tissue culture** can be used to take a small group of plant cells and use these to grow a whole new plant.
- In animals, the cells of **embryos** can be divided up to produce several identical embryos which are transplanted into **surrogate** animals.
- In **adult cell cloning**, a nucleus from an egg cell is removed and replaced with the nucleus from an adult cell.
- The resulting individual is identical to the adult from which it was cloned.

 TOP TIP Embryo transplants can be used to help breed endangered species by transplanting the embryos into non-endangered surrogate animals.

Now Try This

d What do you know about cloning? Are the following statements true (T) or false (F)?

Cloning can only be carried out in plants. _____

Cloning produces individuals that are genetically identical. _____

Clones will always look exactly the same as each other. _____

Identical twins are examples of clones. _____

Cloning can be useful. _____

Cloned individuals are always less healthy. _____

Homework

10 Explain why a breeder of racehorses might want to use embryo transplantation.

11 Write a paragraph to explain your views on adult cell cloning.

12 Why do you think some people are against cloning?

Evolution and extinction

ADAPTATION AND SURVIVAL

- Plants and animals require supplies of materials, such as food and oxygen, from their environment in order to survive.
- There are never enough of these materials to go around, so organisms **compete** for the available resources.
- Plants and animals have special features which make them well suited to their environment and more likely to survive.
- **Adaptations** may be behavioural, for example huddling in penguins.
- In cold climates, a small surface area to volume ratio helps animals reduce heat loss.

- In hot climates, cacti reduce water loss by having spines instead of leaves.
- Adaptation allows species to **evolve**, as the best adapted organisms are more likely to survive and reproduce.

Now Try This

a Complete the passage by filling in the missing words.

Adaptations are _____ or _____ which make an organism well _____ to its _____. This makes it more likely that they will _____ and _____.

Surface area to volume ratio is the amount of skin or surface an animal has over its body compared to its body size or volume.

Homework

1 Describe how a camel is adapted to live in desert conditions.
2 Design an animal to live in a polar environment.
3 Write a paragraph, using examples, to explain what competition is.

THEORIES OF EVOLUTION

- **Fossils** are the remains of plants and animals that lived millions of years ago.
- Fossils form when dead organisms are buried soon after death for millions of years, preventing decay.
- Similarities between fossils and living species provide evidence for **evolution**.
- Jean-Baptiste Lamarck thought that an organism's environment caused it to change, and that these changes were passed on to offspring.
- Darwin later put forward his theory of evolution by **natural selection**.

Evolution is a process of gradual, continuous change in the characteristics of organisms over long periods of time.

Now Try This

b What do you know about evolution? Are the following statements true (T) or false (F)?

Evolution is still going on today. _____

Most of the species that have ever existed are now extinct. _____

Evolution only occurs in animals. _____

Plants decay and so cannot form fossils. _____

Fossils prove that evolution has occurred. _____

Some people do not believe in evolution. _____

Homework

4 Write a paragraph to explain how Lamarck accounted for long necks in giraffes.
5 Why is the fossil record incomplete?
6 Explain why Lamarck's theory of evolution is incorrect.

NATURAL SELECTION

- **Charles Darwin** observed how different species are adapted to their **environments**.
- Individuals differ within populations and some are better **adapted** than others.
- Those that are best adapted are more likely to survive long enough to reproduce.
- They reproduce and pass on the **characteristics** that enable them to survive.
- He called this '**survival of the fittest**'.
- We now know that differences between individuals are due to **genes**, which are passed on to offspring.
- In recent years **natural selection** has caused the evolution of antibiotic-resistant strains of bacteria.

 TOP TIP Genetic mutations may create new genes that make organisms more likely to survive.

Now Try This

c Rearrange the following sentences to describe how natural selection occurs.

  i The genes that helped them survive are passed on to the offspring.

  ii There is variation within a population.

  iii The best adapted individuals survive and reproduce.

  iv Some individuals are better adapted than others.

  v The offspring are well adapted to the environment.

Homework

7 Write a paragraph to explain how antibiotic resistance arises in bacteria.

8 Why was Darwin's theory not accepted straight away?

9 Explain, using the giraffe as an example, how natural selection occurs.

EXTINCTION

- If an organism dies out completely it is said to be **extinct**.
- Extinction happens when an organism cannot adapt to its environment.
- If the environment changes significantly there may not be any individuals who can survive.
- A new **disease** or **predator** may kill all organisms in a **population**.
- A new **competitor** may be better adapted to their habitat and out-compete them for vital resources.
- **Habitat** destruction due to human activity may cause the extinction of some **endangered species** in the near future.

 TOP TIP Existing diseases and predators do not cause extinction as populations are adapted to these environmental factors.

Now Try This

d Which of the following are possible causes of extinction?

  i A tsunami which submerges a whole island. ☐

  ii A harsh winter. ☐

  iii Clearing large areas of forest. ☐

  iv Use of pesticides on crops. ☐

  v An outbreak of an existing disease. ☐

  vi An earthquake. ☐

Homework

10 Describe **two** ways in which humans can contribute to the extinction of a species.

11 Use the Internet to find a list of endangered species.

12 Research and write a paragraph on why the Dodo became extinct.

Our impact on the environment

TOO MANY PEOPLE

- The human **population** has risen rapidly over the last 300 years and is still increasing.
- People are living longer as there are fewer deaths from starvation and disease.
- An increased population places greater demands on the Earth's **resources**.
- More land is used for agriculture and building.
- **Fertilisers** and **pesticides** used in agriculture pollute the environment.
- More **waste** is produced and **raw materials** such as **fossil fuels** are being used up.
- Land which was once a **habitat** for plants or animals is no longer available.

Now Try This

a Complete the passage by filling in the missing words.

The human population is _____. People are living _____ as improved _____ means better food, and better _____ care means fewer deaths from _____. More land is now being used for _____ and _____ and more _____ is being produced.

Homework

1 Explain why population growth is greater in the developing world.
2 List **three** natural resources that humans are using up.
3 Explain how an increasing population leads to habitat destruction.

POLLUTION AND ACID RAIN

- **Pollution** is caused by improper handling of waste from human activity.
- Water may be polluted with **sewage** or **fertilisers** from agriculture.
- Air may be polluted with smoke and chemicals from burning fuels.
- Land may be polluted with **pesticides** and **herbicides** from agriculture.
- **Sulfur dioxide** and **oxides of nitrogen** are released from power stations and motor vehicles emit exhaust fumes.
- These gases dissolve in moisture in the air to produce **acid rain**.
- Acid rain damages trees and buildings. It also makes lakes acidic which kills off aquatic life.

 TOP TIP Living organisms can be used as indicators of pollution, for example, lichens are sensitive to the amount of sulfur dioxide in the air.

Now Try This

b Which kind of pollution (air, water, land) do the following cause?

Driving a motor vehicle _____

Using fertilisers in farming _____

Dumping sewage _____

Burning a coal fire _____

Using electricity at home _____

Failing to recycle domestic rubbish _____

Use of pesticides in agriculture _____

Homework

4 Explain how wasting electricity at home can result in pollution.
5 Write a paragraph about what humans should do to reduce pollution.
6 Make a list of all the things you could do to reduce your contribution to pollution.

GLOBAL WARMING

- **Carbon dioxide** and **methane** in the atmosphere prevent heat escaping from the Earth's surface.
- Some heat is re-radiated back to the Earth, which keeps it warm.
- This '**greenhouse effect**' maintains a temperature warm enough to sustain life.
- Atmospheric carbon dioxide levels are increasing due to burning **fossil fuels** and **deforestation**.
- An increased greenhouse effect may be causing the Earth's atmosphere to heat up. This is known as **global warming**.
- Global warming may cause climate changes and a rise in sea level.
- Methane produced by herds of cattle and rice fields is also a '**greenhouse gas**'.

 TOP TIP Deforestation reduces the rate of carbon dioxide use by plants in photosynthesis, and also destroys habitats.

Now Try This

c Complete the passage by filling in the missing words.

Carbon dioxide and methane are examples of _____ gases. They prevent _____ escaping the Earth's surface. Some of this heat is _____ back to Earth. This keeps the Earth's surface _____ than it would otherwise be. An increased _____ effect may be leading to _____ _____. Human activities such as burning _____ _____ and _____ are contributing to this problem.

Homework

7 Explain the difference between the greenhouse effect and global warming.

8 List **five** things that could be done to reduce global warming.

9 Write a paragraph about the possible effects of global warming.

SUSTAINABLE DEVELOPMENT

- Improving the quality of life without damaging the environment and compromising future generations is called **sustainable development**.
- This involves reducing pollution and conserving the Earth's resources.
- Sustainable development requires management at local, regional and global levels.
- Measures that can be taken include:
  - **recycling** of resources such as paper, glass and aluminium.
  - use of **renewable energy** resources, such as **wind power** and **solar power**.
  - energy-efficient homes, using insulation and double glazing.
  - reducing the use of motor vehicles by walking, cycling or using public transport.
  - planting a new tree for each tree cut down.
  - quotas on pollution imposed on governments.

 TOP TIP Most of the electricity you use is generated by a power station that burns fossil fuels!

Now Try This

d Are the following energy resources renewable (R) or non-renewable (N)?

Fossil fuels (coal, oil, gas) _____

Wind turbines _____

Nuclear power _____

Wave power _____

Hydroelectric power _____

Solar power _____

Tidal power _____

Homework

10 List **five** ways in which you could reduce your energy consumption at home.

11 Make a list of all the rubbish you produce in a day which could be recycled.

12 Explain why sustainable development is difficult to manage at a global level.

All about atoms

ATOMS AND ELEMENTS

- All substances are made of **atoms**.
- An **element** has only one type of atom.
- There are about 100 different elements which are all shown in the **periodic table**.
- The **groups** contain elements with similar **properties**.
- Different atoms have different **symbols**. Na is for sodium and Cl is for chlorine.
- An atom has a small **nucleus** at its centre and this is surrounded by **electrons**.

 TOP TIP If you have only **one type of atom** present then you have only **one** element.

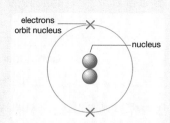

electrons orbit nucleus

nucleus

Now try this

a Match the definition on the left-hand side to the correct word on the right-hand side.

i Elements are made of one type only.

ii For calcium it is Ca.

iii Part of the periodic table where elements have similar properties.

iv There are about 100 of them.

v Small central part of atom.

vi Surround the central nucleus.

nucleus

atom

symbol

group

electrons

elements

Homework

1 Draw and label a diagram of an atom which contains six protons, six neutrons and six electrons.

2 Use the Internet to find out the origins of **20** element names.

3 See if you can find out which country links the elements yttrium and ytterbium.

MAKING COMPOUNDS

- A **compound** forms when **elements** react together.
- When a compound forms, this involves the **electrons** from the outer part of the atoms.
- In some cases, different atoms share their electrons to make **chemical bonds**.
- In other cases, bonds are made by atoms giving and taking electrons.
- When chemicals react, no atoms are lost or gained, they are just rearranged.
- We can write **balanced equations** showing the atoms involved in a **chemical reaction**.

 TOP TIP We balance equations to show that when chemicals react, no atoms are lost or gained.

Now try this

b Which of these is an element?

H_2O CO_2 CO   Co

c Which of these is a compound?

Ca   Ni   NO   H

d Which one of these statements is true?

- Atoms are shared when compounds form.
- One type of atom changes to another in chemical reactions.
- Balanced equations show that atoms are not lost or gained in chemical reactions.
- When compounds form this always involves electrons being shared.

Homework

4 Explain why we must balance chemical equations.

5 What is the difference between an element and a compound?

6 Construct a table to show **five** elements and **five** compounds that can be made from them.

USING SYMBOLS AND EQUATIONS

- To show what is happening during a chemical reaction we use different symbols, for example + and →.
- The **formula** of a compound shows the number and type of atoms that are joined together to make the compound.
- The formula Na_2SO_4 tells us there are two sodium atoms, one sulfur atom and four oxygen atoms in the compound sodium sulfate.
- The equation $2H_2 + O_2 \rightarrow 2H_2O$ tells us that two hydrogen molecules react with one oxygen molecule to make two water molecules.

Now try this

e Complete the following statements.

To show '**reacts with**' we use the symbol _____.

To show '**makes**' we use the symbol _____.

The formula $NaNO_3$ tells us the compound contains _____ sodium atom, _____ nitrogen atom and three _____ atoms.

Homework

7 Explain what the formula NH_4NO_3 tells us.

8 Explain what the formula $Ca(OH)_2$ tells us.

9 Explain what the equation $H_2 + Cl_2 \rightarrow 2HCl$ tells us.

LIMESTONE

- Limestone contains the compound calcium carbonate.
- Calcium carbonate has the formula $CaCO_3$.
- Limestone is quarried and can be used as a building material.
- Calcium carbonate can be decomposed by heating it. This process is known as thermal decomposition.
- When it decomposes, calcium carbonate makes calcium oxide (quicklime) and carbon dioxide.
- Limestone and its products have many uses, including making slaked lime (calcium hydroxide), mortar, cement, concrete and glass.

Quarrying limestone

Now try this

f Look at the following statements and write **T** if they are **true** and **F** if they are **false**. If you think a statement is false then say why you think it is wrong.

Statement	T or F	If false, why is it wrong?
i Calcium carbonate contains one calcium atom, one carbon atom and three oxygen atoms.		
ii Limestone is quarried as it has few uses.		
iii Limestone can be made using glass.		
iv Limestone's common name is quicklime.		

Homework

10 Limestone is mainly calcium carbonate. What other rocks are made of calcium carbonate?

11 Investigate other uses of limestone apart from those shown above. How many can you find?

12 Use the Internet to find out **two** counties in Britain where limestone can be quarried.

Metals from ores

ORES

- An **ore** contains enough **metal** to make money from extracting the metal.
- An ore which it is not currently **economical** to exploit may become useful if the metal becomes more scarce.
- We can find **unreactive** metals such as **gold** in the Earth, in the form of the metal itself.
- Most metals are found combined with other elements and chemical reactions are needed to extract these metals.
- Low reactivity metals, such as **iron**, can be **extracted** by heating their oxides with carbon.
- Iron oxide can be reduced to iron in a **blast furnace** when carbon takes the oxygen away from the iron.

 TOP TIP Metals lower than carbon in the reactivity series can be extracted from their ores by heating with carbon.

Now try this

a Match the definition on the left-hand side to the correct word on the right-hand side.

i A metal that can be found uncombined in the Earth.	iron oxide
ii A metal usually found combined in the Earth.	ore
iii A non-metal often used to extract metal.	carbon
iv A compound that is used in a blast furnace.	gold
v A rock that contains enough metal to extract and make money.	iron

Homework

1. Explain in your own words what an ore is.
2. Look on the Internet for a diagram of a blast furnace and label it to show how it works.
3. Name **three** metals that can be found uncombined in the Earth's crust.

IRON AND ITS ALLOYS

- **Iron** from the **blast furnace** contains 4 % impurities, which makes it **brittle**.
- Removing the impurities produces pure iron, which can be bent and shaped easily.
- In metals such as iron, the atoms are arranged in layers which can slide over each other. This is why these metals can bend.
- Most iron is converted into **steel**, an **alloy** of iron, which contains carbon and other metals.
- Adding different atoms to iron distorts the layers and makes it harder for them to slide over each other. This makes the alloys stronger and harder than pure iron.
- **Low carbon steels** bend easily. **High carbon steel** is very hard. **Stainless steel** does not rust.

 TOP TIP An alloy is a mixture of metals.

Now try this

b Complete the following sentences by filling in the missing words.

Iron from the blast furnace which is only _____ % pure is very _____. When impurities are removed, the pure iron is very _____. Small amounts of carbon may be added to iron to make the _____ low carbon steel. This alloy can easily be bent and shaped. High carbon steels are much _____. Another useful alloy of iron is stainless steel, which does not _____.

Homework

4. Use the Internet to find out the composition of some alloys of iron.
5. Draw a diagram to show why iron becomes harder when carbon is added.
6. Use the Internet to find out why the Sheffield United football team are called 'The Blades'.

See pages 122–141 of Collins GCSE Science

THE TRANSITION OF METALS

- The elements in the central block of the periodic table (for example, nickel, iron, titanium, copper, gold and silver) are the **transition metals**.
- Like most metals, they are strong and can be bent and hammered into shape.
- This makes them useful for making structures such as bridges.
- Like most metals they are also good **conductors** of heat and electricity.
- **Copper** is used for wiring and plumbing.
- Copper is usually extracted using **electrolysis**.
- Copper ores are not plentiful and low grade ores (not useful previously) are now being exploited commercially.
- The impact on the environment is reduced as there is less new mining.

Copper piping.

Now try this

c Circle the correct answer in each group of four.

i A transition metal
  - titanium
  - aluminium
  - sodium
  - magnesium

ii A property of metals
  - brittle
  - bend
  - insulate
  - don't corrode

iii Copper isn't used for making …
  - wiring
  - pipes
  - bridges
  - plumbing fittings

Homework

7 Make an illustrated poster all about copper.

8 Find out where copper mines are or have been in Britain.

9 Find out which Mediterranean island gives copper its name, using an online periodic table.

OTHER ALLOYS

- Pure gold, aluminium and copper are too soft for many uses, so they are made into **alloys** by mixing them with similar metals.
- Some alloys are known as **smart alloys** and these regain their shape after they have been bent, squashed or twisted.
- **Aluminium** is a very useful metal (especially when alloyed) as it has a **low density** and does not rust.
- **Titanium** is another lightweight metal which resists **corrosion**.
- Aluminium and titanium cannot be extracted by heating with carbon.
- Lots of energy and many chemical processes are therefore needed to extract these metals.
- This means that these metals are expensive and, like many metals, it is economical and environmentally friendly to **recycle** them.

Now try this

d Say whether these statements are true or false in the second column. If false, explain why in the third column.

Statement	T or F	If false, why is it wrong?
i Smart alloys have shape memory.		
ii Titanium has a low density but corrodes.		
iii Pure gold is too hard for many uses.		
iv Aluminium is recycled as it is expensive to extract.		
v Aluminium is expensive as it is a limited resource.		

Homework

10 Find out about a smart alloy and write about it in your own words.

11 Explain why titanium and aluminium are such useful metals.

12 List as many uses for aluminium as you can.

Crude oil

CRUDE OIL IS A MIXTURE

- **Crude oil** is a **mixture** containing many different compounds.
- In a mixture, the **elements** or **compounds** are not chemically combined with each other.
- The components of a mixture can be separated using the physical differences between them.
- Each of the components of a mixture keeps its own properties.
- The different compounds in crude oil can be separated by **fractional distillation**.

 TOP TIP Fractional distillation works because the different compounds in crude oil have different boiling points.

Now try this

a Complete the following sentences by filling in the missing words.

Crude oil is a _____ of different _____. The different compounds can be separated using _____ _____ because each of the compounds has a different _____ _____.

Homework

1 Use examples to explain the differences between a mixture, a compound and an element.

2 Construct a table that shows **three** examples of a mixture, a compound and an element.

3 Explain why fractional distillation is able to separate out the components of crude oil.

ALKANES

- Most of the **compounds** in **crude oil** are compounds called **hydrocarbons**.
- A hydrocarbon is a compound made only of the elements **hydrogen** and **carbon**.
- Most of the hydrocarbons in crude oil are **saturated** hydrocarbons.
- These saturated hydrocarbons are called **alkanes**.
- Alkanes have the general formula C_nH_{2n+2}.
- Alkane molecules can be shown in the following ways:

Now try this

b Circle the correct answer.

i Alkanes are

compounds   mixtures   elements

ii Alkanes have the general formula

$C_{2n}+2H_n$ C_nH_{2n+2} C_nH_{2n}

iii Alkanes are

unsaturated   saturated   saturation

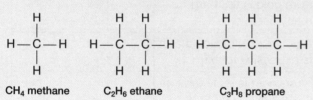

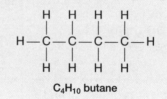

CH₄ methane   C₂H₆ ethane   C₃H₈ propane   C₄H₁₀ butane

 TOP TIP In an alkane every carbon atom must have four single bonds.

Homework

4 What do you understand by the term hydrocarbon?

5 What name is given to a hydrocarbon with four carbons in it?

6 Work out the formula of an alkane with 22 carbons in it.

FRACTIONAL DISTILLATION OF CRUDE OIL

- **Crude oil** can be separated into **fractions** by **fractional distillation**.
- Each fraction is still a mixture, but the compounds in each fraction have a similar number of carbons.
- To separate crude oil it is first heated.
- This makes the compounds evaporate.
- The gases are then allowed to cool and they condense at different temperatures.
- The way molecules behave depends on their size.
- The size of a molecule determines whether or not it will be a good fuel.

Now try this

c Number the list correctly so that it is in the right order to show fractional distillation.

☐ The gases are cooled.

☐ You end up with different fractions containing similar numbers of molecules.

☐ This evaporates all of the compounds.

☐ Crude oil is heated.

☐ The different molecules condense at different temperatures.

Homework

7 Make a poster and illustrate it to show how fractional distillation works.

8 Explain what is meant by the term 'fraction'.

9 Use the Internet to find out what 'Brent Crude' is.

WHAT FORMS WHEN FUELS BURN?

- Most **fuels** contain carbon and/or hydrogen.
- When these fuels burn, the carbon forms carbon dioxide, CO_2 (which causes **global warming**) and the hydrogen forms water vapour, H_2O.
- Sometimes **solid particles** form and these cause **global dimming**.
- Some fuels contain sulfur (S), as an impurity. In vehicle fuels the sulfur is removed before the fuel is burnt.
- If not removed, these fuels release **sulfur dioxide** (SO_2) as well as CO_2 and H_2O.
- Sulfur dioxide causes **acid rain**. In power stations, it must be removed from the gases before they leave the chimney.

Now try this

d Answer these questions using one of the following answers: S, CO_2, SO_2, H_2O, solid particles.

The two gases made when a hydrocarbon burns: _____

The gas that causes acid rain: _____

The gas that must be removed from power stations after fuels are burnt: _____

The substance present as an impurity in some hydrocarbon fuels: _____

The gas made when hydrogen fuel burns: _____

The gas made when carbon burns: _____

The substance that causes global dimming: _____

Homework

10 Make a poster to show how all the pollutants mentioned above are formed.

11 Which pollutant causes global dimming?

12 Find out how sulfur dioxide is removed from power station chimneys.

Cracking and polymers

CRACKING HYDROCARBONS

- As a result of **fractional distillation** we end up with too many of the larger molecules and not enough of the smaller molecules.
- The large molecules can be 'cracked' to break them into smaller, more useful molecules. This is known as **thermal decomposition**.
- Cracking involves passing the heated vapours of large molecules over a hot **catalyst**.
- Cracking always makes smaller **alkanes** and **alkenes**.
- Alkenes are **unsaturated hydrocarbons** with the general formula C_nH_{2n}.
- Alkenes can be shown as: C_3H_6 or

Cracking always makes at least one alkene and an alkane.

Now try this

a Circle the correct answer.

i Cracking does not need
    heat   a catalyst   small hydrocarbons

ii Alkenes have the general formula
    C_nH_n $C_{2n}H_n$ C_nH_{2n}

iii An example of an alkene is
    C_4H_{10} C_7H_{14} C_2H_2

iv Alkenes are not
    molecules   hydrocarbons   saturated

v The structural formula of propene is

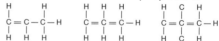

vi Cracking makes
    big molecules   small molecules   crude oil

Homework

1 Draw a flow chart to show how propene (C_3H_6) is obtained from crude oil.
2 Explain why cracking is useful.
3 Draw a diagram to show a molecule of butene, C_4H_8.

USING THE PRODUCTS OF CRACKING

- Some of the products that are made from **cracking** are used as **fuels**.
- This is because cracking makes more of the smaller molecules that burn well.
- **Ethene** (C_2H_4) reacts with steam (H_2O) in the presence of a **catalyst** to make **ethanol**.
- Good quality ethanol can be made quickly by this method.
- Making ethanol in this way (as opposed to making it from fermenting sugar) means a non-renewable source is being used.
- **Alkenes** can be used to make **polymers** such as poly(ethene) and poly(propene).

Now try this

b Complete the sentences by filling in the missing words.

Alkenes react with _____ in the presence of a _____ to make compounds called alcohols. For example, _____ can be reacted with _____ in the presence of a catalyst to make ethanol. Alkenes are also useful because they can be used to make _____ such as _____ and poly(propene). As well as making alkenes, cracking also makes smaller _____, which can be used as _____.

Homework

4 How is ethanol made from ethene?
5 Why is making ethanol by this method better than making it by fermentation?
6 Why is making ethanol by this method not as good as making it by fermentation?

FROM MONOMER TO POLYMER

- In order to make a **polymer** the **monomer** must have a **double bond**. It must be **unsaturated**.
- When a small molecule such as **ethene** is used to make poly(ethene) we say that ethene is a monomer.
- When many thousands of monomers are added together, a polymer is made.
- When many thousands of ethene monomers are reacted together, the polymer poly(ethene) forms.
- When many thousands of propene monomers are reacted together, the polymer poly(propene) forms.

Now try this

c Link the monomer to the polymer.

i   ethene   poly(propene)

ii C_3H_6 poly(styrene)

iii styrene   poly(butene)

iv C_4H_8 poly(ethene)

Homework

7   Explain why C_2H_6 cannot be used to make polymers.

8   Draw a cartoon, a picture or make a model to show how polymers form.

9   Use the Internet to find the monomer that is used to make PVC.

PROPERTIES AND USES OF POLYMERS

- The way in which a particular **polymer** behaves depends on what the **monomer** is and the conditions it was made under.
- Slime can be made from the polymer poly(ethenol), which is also known as PVA. The **viscosity** (how easily it flows) can be varied according to the conditions it is made under.
- Polymers have many uses including: packaging materials, waterproof fabric coatings, dental polymers for fillings, dressings for wounds and hydrogels.
- **Smart materials** such as 'shape memory plastics' are also being developed.
- There are so many **plastics** now in use that disposal has become a problem.
- It is desirable to **recycle** plastics but they are difficult to separate from each other before recycling.
- We can dispose of polymers by burning them but some may release toxic fumes.
- Polymers are not **biodegradable** and therefore **landfill sites** are not a solution to the problem of disposal.

Now try this

d Say whether you think these statements are true or false. If a statement is false, explain why.

Statement	T or F	If false, why is it wrong?
i Plastics are easy to recycle.		
ii Plastics are finding more and more uses.		
iii A good way to dispose of plastics is to burn them.		
iv Plastics cannot be broken down by bacteria.		

Homework

10 Bring in **three** different polymers from home and add them to a collection at school.

11 Explain why disposing of polymers is such a problem.

12 Use the Internet to find out why 'shape memory plastics' are clever and write about them.

Food chemistry

PLANT OILS

- Many of the oils we use are **extracted** from nuts, seeds and fruits.
- To extract the oil, the plant material is crushed to squeeze it out. In some cases the oil is separated off by **distillation**. Water and impurities are removed.
- Vegetable oils are useful fuels and foods as they contain a lot of **energy**.
- Oils are a useful part of our diet as they provide us with **nutrients**.
- Oils do not dissolve in water, but we can make them mix by turning them into **emulsions**.
- Emulsions are thicker than either the oil or water on their own and they have better texture, appearance and ability to coat.
- Two emulsions you know of are salad dressing and ice cream.

Now try this

a Complete the sentences by filling in the missing words.

Plant oils are useful in our diet as they provide _____ and _____. Oil and vinegar will not mix so we add an emulsifier such as _____ to make them join together and form an _____. Salad dressing is better than oil and vinegar separately because it can _____ the food more easily and has a thicker _____.

Homework

1 Go home and ask your parents what different types of oil they use in the kitchen.
2 Try to make an emulsion at home using vinegar and oil. Try different emulsifiers.
3 Write a report of your experiment.

SATURATED OR UNSATURATED?

- Vegetable oils are **unsaturated**.
- This means they contain carbon–carbon double bonds like the **alkenes**.
- You can show that an oil is unsaturated by reacting it with bromine or iodine.
- The **iodine number** indicates the number of carbon–carbon double bonds present.
- We can react vegetable oils with hydrogen at about 60 °C with a nickel catalyst present. This makes a **hard fat** (margarine).
- The hardened oils have higher melting points so they are solids at room temperature. This means they can be spread on foods and are easier to use for cake-making.

 TOP TIP To test for unsaturation just add bromine or iodine solution and if they lose their colour, you know there were double bonds present.

Now try this

b Match the statements on the right-hand side with the type of hydrocarbon.

methane

C_3H_6

unsaturated   decolourises bromine

iodine solution stays brown

C_3H_8

contains only C–C single bonds

saturated   contains at least one C–C double bond

general formula is C_nH_{2n}

Homework

4 How do you make margarine from vegetable oils?
5 What is meant by a catalyst?
6 Explain the benefits of hardening oils.

FOOD ADDITIVES

- **Additives** may be added to make food stay fresh for longer.
- Additives may be added to improve the appearance or taste of a food.
- Additives must be listed with the ingredients.
- Some additives have **E-numbers**.
- The presence of additives can be identified using **chemical analysis**.
- We can identify added (or natural) colours using **chromatography**.
- To obtain a chromatogram like the one below, you draw a pencil line near the bottom of the chromatography paper. Place a few drops of an **extract** from each food sample on the line and then dip the paper in some **solvent** in a beaker.

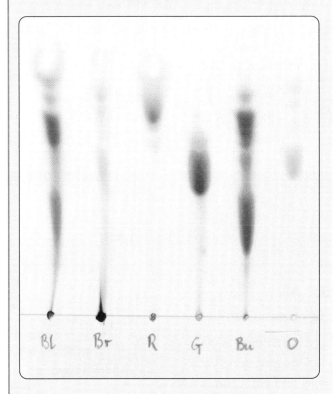

 TOP TIP Once you understand how to 'read' this chromatogram you should be able to understand any other chromatogram.

Now try this

c The chromatogram shown below has been made to analyse colours used in frozen peas. Six samples were tested. Look at the chromatogram and answer the questions that follow.

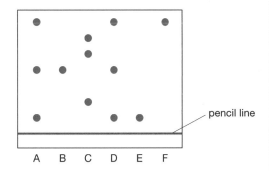

i Which samples contained at least **three** different dyes? _____

ii Which samples probably contained only a single dye? _____

iii Which samples contained the same dye as in B? _____

iv Which sample contained different dyes from all of the rest? _____

Homework

7 Find the names of **five** different food additives by reading labels on food in your kitchen.

8 Use the Internet to find out what is so bad about the food additive E-102.

9 Use the information you have found to make an information leaflet about additive E-102.

The Earth and its atmosphere

THE EARTH'S CRUST

- Scientists used to think that the Earth's surface features were due to uneven shrinking of the Earth as it cooled down following its formation.
- We now know that ideas about **tectonic plates** explain the presence of some of the Earth's physical features, for example, mountains and oceans.
- The top part of the Earth (the **crust** and top part of the **mantle**) is broken into large pieces called tectonic plates.
- These plates move at speeds of several centimetres a year.
- They move because they lie above **convection currents** in the mantle.
- The heat that causes convection in the mantle comes from **radioactive decay** processes.
- The movements can, at times, be sudden and may cause disasters such as **earthquakes**.
- Earthquakes and **volcanic eruptions** occur along the edges of plates where they meet.

Now try this

a Match the descriptions on the right-hand side with the words on the left-hand side.

i tectonic plate	a few metres every century
	occur at plate boundaries
ii radioactive decay	provides energy for convection currents in the mantle
iii plate movement	
iv volcanoes	large piece of Earth's crust and upper mantle
v Earth cooling	has occurred since its formation

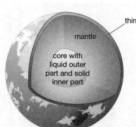

thin rocky crust
mantle
core with liquid outer part and solid inner part

Homework

1. Which layers of the Earth form tectonic plates?
2. What causes tectonic plates to move?
3. Before the theory of plate tectonics, how did scientists think mountains were formed?

THE EARTH'S ATMOSPHERE

- The **atmosphere** today has been much the same for the last 200 million years.
- It contains about 80% **nitrogen**.
- It contains about 20% oxygen.
- There are small amounts of other gases including **water vapour**, **carbon dioxide** and **noble gases** (mainly **argon**).

Now try this

b Which gas is being described?

i Forms 80% of the air around you. _____

ii Forms 20% of the air around you. _____

iii Is present in air and easily forms a liquid on cooling. _____

iv Present in air in tiny amounts and we exhale it. _____

v The amount in air depends on the temperature. _____

Homework

4. Draw a pie chart to show the composition of the Earth's atmosphere.
5. Find uses for all the gases in your pie chart.
6. Why is it that lots of people don't know that nitrogen is in the air?

USES OF NOBLE GASES

- The **noble gases** are in **group 0** of the **periodic table**.
- The noble gases are extremely **unreactive**.
- Noble gases can be used in light bulbs (filament lamps) and discharge lamps, like neon lights and strip lights.
- **Helium**, another noble gas, is much less dense than air and can be used in balloons.

Now try this

c Which gas is being described?

  i Can be used in discharge tubes. _____

  ii A noble gas not used in balloons. _____

  iii The lightest noble gas. _____

 The use of noble gases depends on the fact that they are not very reactive.

Homework

7 Make an information poster or PowerPoint show about the noble gases.

8 Find out why the noble gases are so unreactive.

9 Some metals are known as 'Noble Metals'. Use the Internet to find out their names.

HOW THE EARTH'S ATMOSPHERE DEVELOPED

- For the first billion years on Earth, there was powerful **volcanic activity** at the surface.
- This released the gases which formed the Earth's early atmosphere.
- The main gas present was **carbon dioxide** (CO_2) and there was no **oxygen** (O_2).
- This is like the atmosphere of Venus and Mars today.
- It is thought that the other gases were **water vapour** (H_2O), small amounts of **ammonia** (NH_3) and **methane** (CH_4).
- As the surface cooled, the water vapour condensed to make the oceans.
- Oxygen only appeared in our atmosphere after plants evolved.
- Carbon dioxide was removed as it became locked up in **sedimentary carbonate rocks** (such as limestone and chalk) and **fossil fuels** (such as oil and coal).
- Recently we have started to release this carbon dioxide by burning large amounts of fossil fuels.

Carbon dioxide locked up millions of years ago is released when we burn this coal.

Now try this

d Answer **UP** or **DOWN** to each of these questions.

Formation of fossil fuels makes CO_2 levels in the atmosphere go _____

Formation of chalk makes CO_2 levels in the atmosphere go _____

Evolution of plants made the amount of O_2 in the atmosphere go _____

Burning fossil fuels makes CO_2 levels in the atmosphere go _____

Condensation of H_2O makes levels of this gas in the atmosphere go _____

Since the first billion years of the Earth's existence, CO_2 levels have gone _____

Since the first billion years of the Earth's existence, NH_3 levels have gone _____

Since the first billion years of the Earth's existence, volcanic activity has gone _____

Global warming would make the level of water vapour in the atmosphere go _____

Homework

10 Which gases were present in the Earth's early atmosphere?

11 Where has all the CO_2 from the Earth's early atmosphere gone?

12 Why is the amount of CO_2 in the atmosphere increasing nowadays?

Thermal energy

THERMAL RADIATION

Now try this

a Which of the following statements are true?

  i Thermal radiation is emitted by rays known as infrared waves. _____

  ii A red-hot oven emits more thermal radiation than when it is cold. _____

  iii Polar bears absorb lots of thermal radiation because of their white fur. _____

  iv An object at –20 °C is warmer than an object at –50 °C. _____

 TOP TIP All bodies emit and absorb thermal radiation.

- **Temperature** is measured with a **thermometer** in **degrees Celsius** (°C).
- The temperature of a body is a measure of its 'hotness'.
- **Energy** can be transferred by **conduction**, **convection** and **radiation**.
- **Thermal radiation** is the transfer of energy by **electromagnetic waves** known as **infrared waves**.
- The infrared radiation emitted by an object (for example, a person) can be detected by a 'thermal imaging camera' or a thermopile.
- The hotter a body is the more energy it radiates as thermal radiation.
- The greater the temperature difference between a body and its surroundings, the greater the rate at which energy is transferred.
- Dark, matt surfaces are good **absorbers** and good **emitters** of thermal radiation.
- Shiny surfaces **reflect** infrared radiation.
- Light, shiny surfaces are poor absorbers and poor emitters of thermal radiation.
- Infrared radiation does not require a medium.

Homework

1 In your own words, describe the difference between temperature and heat.
2 Make a list of objects emitting infrared radiation in your house.
3 Write a short paragraph on the properties of infrared radiation as an electromagnetic wave.

CONVECTION

- In **convection**, energy transfer occurs due to the movement of a **fluid** (liquid or gas).
- Convection can only happen in fluids (liquids and gases) where the atoms or particles are free to move.
- In convection, hot liquid (or air) rises and is replaced by falling colder liquid (or air). This gives rise to **convection currents**.

Now try this

b Which of the following statements is/are correct?

i Metals cannot transfer heat by convection because the particles cannot move. _____

ii Convection is not possible in a vacuum because there are no particles. _____

iii Convection is impossible in water. _____

Homework

4 Use a labelled diagram to explain how convection currents are set up in a kettle full of water.

5 Describe how a 'radiator' at one end of a room heats the air in that room.

6 Make a list of examples of convection currents.

CONDUCTION

- Good **thermal conductors** allow easy transfer of heat energy.
- Poor thermal conductors are known as **insulators**, for example glass and plastic.
- In a solid, thermal energy is transferred by atomic or particle **vibrations**.
- **Metals** are good thermal conductors because the energy is transferred by both atomic vibrations and by free electrons.
- The transfer of energy by the free electrons is faster than by atomic vibrations.
- **Non-metals** (for example, plastic, wood) are poor thermal conductors because they have fewer free electrons.
- **Liquids** (for example, water) and **gases** (for example, air) are poor thermal conductors or good thermal insulators.
- Many insulators in the home contain trapped air (for example, loft insulation or fibreglass, double glazing in windows and cavity-wall insulation foam).
- A **vacuum** is a perfect insulator because there are no particles.

Now try this

c Cross out the incorrect word in each statement, leaving the correct word.

i Air is a good **conductor/insulator**.

ii Water is a **poor/good** thermal conductor.

iii Solids are good conductors of heat because the particles are **close together/far apart**.

 Good thermal insulators are poor thermal conductors.

Homework

7 Make a table of materials under the headings 'good insulators' and 'good conductors'.

8 In your own words, explain why metals are better thermal conductors than non-metals like plastic.

9 Make a list of insulators in your home that minimise the loss of heat.

Efficient use of energy

ENERGY

- Some examples of energy:
  - **heat** energy
  - **chemical** energy
  - **electrical** energy
  - **light** energy
  - **wave** energy
  - **sound** energy
  - **nuclear** energy
  - **kinetic** energy
  - **potential** (stored) energy.
- **Conservation** of energy:
  Energy cannot be created or destroyed. The total energy always remains the same.
- Energy can only be **transformed** from one form to another. For example, a light bulb changes electrical energy into light energy and heat energy.

- The energy not used by a device is known as 'wasted energy'.
- The wasted energy is often **transferred** to the surroundings as heat energy.
- The kinetic energy of the atoms increases when heat energy is transferred to the surroundings.
- input energy = wasted energy + useful energy
- Having loft insulation, cavity-wall insulation, double glazing and draught proofing can reduce energy losses from homes.

Now try this

a **Complete the sentences.**

The useful energy for a car is its k_____ energy. This energy comes from the c_____ energy of the fuel. Almost half of the input energy from the fuel is wasted as h_____ in the moving parts of the car as exhaust gases.

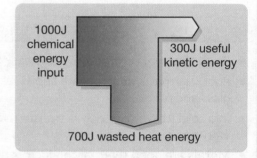

A *Sankey diagram for a car.*

 Energy is measured in joules (J).

Homework

1 Draw a mind map for 'energy'.
2 In your own words, state the principle of conservation of energy and give examples.
3 Give **five** examples of transformation of energy by devices.

ENERGY, WORK AND POWER

- **Work done** is measured in **joules** (J).
- work done = force × distance moved in the direction of the force
- **energy transfer** = work done
- **Power** is measured in **watts** (W).
- $\text{power} = \dfrac{\text{work done}}{\text{time}}$ or $\text{power} = \dfrac{\text{energy transfer}}{\text{time}}$
- One watt is equal to one joule per second.
- A power of 60 W means 60 J of work done per second.

 Energy and work are both measured in joules (J).

Now try this

b Match the beginnings and endings to make complete sentences.

Beginning	Ending
i No work is done on an object if it	second.
ii Power is measured in	joules.
iii Work is measured in	watts.
iv 100 W means 100 J of energy transferred every	remains stationary.

Homework

4 Make a list of the typical power rating of the devices in your home, for example, TV or lamp.

5 Use the Internet to research and write about the energy available from some named chocolate bars.

6 Make a list of all the quantities and their units.

EFFICIENCY

- **efficiency** $= \dfrac{\text{useful energy transferred by device}}{\text{total energy supplied to the device}}$
- The efficiency of a device can be written as a percentage.
- For example, a crane lifts a large tank of water. The total chemical energy supplied to the engine of the crane is 200 000 J. The final potential energy of the water tank is 80 000 J. What is the efficiency of the engine?

$$\text{efficiency} = \frac{80\,000}{200\,000} = 0.40$$

$$\text{efficiency} = 0.40 \times 100 = 40\,\%$$

60 % of the **input energy** is wasted energy (most likely as heat energy).

- A device is more efficient when a greater percentage of the energy is usefully transformed by the device.

 Nothing can be more than 100% efficient.

Now try this

c Which of the following statements is/are correct?

  i Efficiency has no units. ☐

  ii For a car that is 30% efficient, 70% of the energy is wasted. ☐

  iii The input electrical energy to a lamp is 100 J. Only 2 J is emitted as light. The efficiency of the lamp is 98%. ☐

Homework

7 In your own words explain why a device with moving parts can never be 100% efficient.

8 Use the energy transfer diagrams given on pages 216 and 217 of the student book to calculate the efficiency of each device.

9 Use the Internet to research the typical efficiencies of modern cars.

Electricity

ELECTRICAL DEVICES ARE USEFUL

- Mains **electricity** is convenient and reliable for our domestic appliances.
- Many devices transform **electrical energy** into other forms, for example, heat, light and sound.
- An electric kettle changes electrical energy into heat energy.
- A hairdryer changes electrical energy into kinetic energy and heat energy.
- A TV changes electrical energy into heat energy, light energy and sound energy.
- **Batteries** allow electrical devices to be portable.
- **Solar energy** and **potential energy** in clockwork springs can be used to charge **rechargeable** batteries.
- An electric current in a device causes heating.
- Large **currents** can cause excessive heating that can lead to accidental fires.

Now try this

a Cross out the incorrect word in each statement, leaving the correct word.

A battery changes chemical energy into **heat/electrical** energy.

A filament lamp transforms electrical energy into heat energy and **chemical/light** energy.

A current in the filament lamp makes it **cold/hot**.

A battery-powered torch is convenient because it is **portable/heavy**.

Homework

1 Write a paragraph on the advantages of using rechargeable batteries in developing countries.
2 Write a paragraph on the advantages and disadvantages of using a mains operated electric power drill.
3 Make a list of items that use batteries.

COST OF ELECTRICITY

- **Power** is often measured in **watts** (W) or **joules per second** (J/s).
- **Electrical power** is defined as the rate of transfer of electrical energy.
- power = $\dfrac{\text{energy transferred}}{\text{time taken}}$
- The electrical energy **transformed** by a device depends on how long it is used for and the **power rating** of the device.
- energy transferred in joules = power in watts × time in seconds
- The **kilowatt hour** (kWh) is a convenient unit of electrical energy.
- 1 kWh is the energy transferred by a 1 kW device working for a time of 1 hour.
- 1 kWh = 3 600 000 J
- electrical energy transformed in kWh = power in kW × time in hours
- The cost of electricity is calculated using the equation:
cost = power in kW × time in hours × cost of 1 kWh

Now try this

b Which of the following statements is/are correct?

i The joule is a unit of energy. ☐

ii The kilowatt hour is a unit of energy. ☐

iii The watt is a unit of energy. ☐

iv Using an appliance for longer will cost more. ☐

 Do not forget that the kWh is a unit of energy.

Homework

4 Explain what is meant by the 'joule' and the 'kilowatt hour'. Explain why it is convenient to use the kWh for domestic billing.

5 Make a list of all the quantities in this section and the appropriate units.

6 Estimate the cost of using your electric kettle during a day.

THE NATIONAL GRID

- The **National Grid** uses transmission cables to distribute electricity between power stations and our homes and factories.
- In a **power station**, **fossil fuel** is burned to heat water in order to produce high-pressured steam. The steam is used to spin **turbines**. The turbines turn the **generators** and this produces **electricity**.
- The **voltage (potential difference)** from the generator is increased from 25 kV to about 400 kV using **step-up transformers**.
- Electricity is transmitted at high voltage to reduce **current** in the cables and hence reduce the energy losses in the transmission cables.
- Before the electricity can be used at our homes it has to be decreased to 240 V using **step-down transformers**.
- Transformers only step-up and step-down **alternating** voltages.

Now try this

c Find the following key words in this wordsearch.

national   grid   voltage
current   cable   loss

V	C	A	K	O	R	G	L
O	A	G	S	S	O	A	P
L	B	N	A	B	N	L	T
T	L	D	L	O	S	S	D
A	E	P	I	C	E	L	I
G	K	T	A	E	E	L	R
E	A	N	E	C	F	N	G
N	T	N	E	R	R	U	C

Homework

7 Draw a block diagram to show how energy from fossil fuels is transformed into electrical energy for use in our homes.

8 Make a list of electrical devices in the home that use step-down transformers.

9 Write a paragraph to explain why electricity is transmitted at high voltages.

Generating electricity

GENERATING ELECTRICITY

- A **dynamo** is a small electrical **generator**.
- In a dynamo or a generator, an electric **current** is **induced** in a **circuit** by moving a **coil** near a **magnet** or by moving a magnet near a coil.
- A generator produces an **alternating potential difference**.
- A generator in a power station consists of a coil of wire rotating between the poles of a magnet. The coil cuts the magnetic field lines and this induces a potential difference.

Now try this

a Circle all the items needed to make a small electric generator.

battery   motor

resistor   coil

magnet   voltmeter

spring   wires

 TOP TIP A generator transforms kinetic energy into electrical energy.

Homework

1 In your own words, describe how a generator produces electricity.

2 Use a diagram to show how an electric generator produces electricity.

3 Draw a labelled diagram of a bicycle dynamo.

RENEWABLE AND NON-RENEWABLE FUELS

- **Non-renewable energy** resources will eventually run out.
- **Fossil fuels** like coal, natural gas and crude oil are non-renewable resources.
- **Nuclear fuels** like uranium and plutonium are non-renewable resources because they will eventually run out.
- **Renewable** resources of energy can be replaced as we use them or are resources that will be available for a very long time.
- **Biomass resources** like wood, straw and manure are renewable resources because they will not run out as long as chopped down trees are replaced.
- Examples of renewable energy resources: biomass, **hydroelectric**, **wind**, **tidal**, **wave**, **geothermal** and **solar**.

Now try this

b Tick (✓) the correct column for each statement.

Fuel	Renewable	Non-renewable
coal	☐	☐
uranium	☐	☐
straw	☐	☐
manure	☐	☐
crude oil	☐	☐

Homework

4 Make a table of renewable sources and non-renewable sources.

5 Explain why wood may be considered as a renewable fuel.

6 Use the Internet to find the percentage of electricity produced in the UK from renewable resources.

POWER STATIONS

- The most common energy sources are coal, oil and gas. These are burned to produce heat.
- In **power stations**, the fuel is burned to heat water. This produces high-pressured steam to spin the **turbines**. The turbines turn the **generators** and this produces **electricity**. The **National Grid** is used to transmit electricity to consumers.
- Some power stations use uranium or plutonium as fuel. **Nuclear fission** reactions produce the heat in nuclear power stations.
- Energy from **renewable energy sources** is used to directly drive the turbines.
- A **wind turbine** changes the **kinetic energy** of the wind into **electrical energy**.
- Electricity can be produced directly from the Sun's radiation using **solar cells**.
- In some volcanic areas, hot water and steam rise to the surface. The steam can be tapped and used to drive turbines. This is **geothermal energy**.

Now try this

c **Fill in the missing words.**

All power stations are designed to produce _____. In a nuclear power station, a fuel like _____ is used to heat the _____ to produce _____. The steam is used to turn the turbines, which in turn spin the generators.

Homework

7 Draw a block diagram to show the stages in the production of electricity in a coal-burning power station.

8 Research and write about how a wind turbine produces energy.

9 Research and write about geothermal energy.

THE ENVIRONMENT

- Fossil fuels are relatively cheap and produce large amounts of electricity. However, they give off harmful gases, like carbon dioxide, that cause **global warming**.
- **Wind turbines** do not produce any polluting waste and can be used in remote areas. However, wind turbines can be an eyesore. They also require lots of space and their electrical power depends on wind speed.
- **Solar cells** have a long life, do not produce polluting waste and require low maintenance. However, the initial cost of solar cells can be quite high.
- **Nuclear power stations** do not produce **greenhouse gases** like carbon dioxide and therefore do not contribute to global warming.
- Nuclear power stations produce **radioactive waste** that can be active for thousands of years.
- **Tidal power** and **wave power** can change the flow of water and destroy local habitats.

Now try this

d **Which of the following statements is/are correct?**

i All fossil fuels release dangerous greenhouse gases. ☐

ii Fossil fuels are very expensive. ☐

iii Global warming may be due to burning fossil fuels. ☐

iv Solar cells work well at night. ☐

Homework

10 Describe the advantages and disadvantages of using fossil fuels.

11 Describe the advantages and disadvantages of having hydroelectric power in the UK.

12 Explain why very few houses in the UK have solar cells to generate electricity.

Electromagnetic waves

UNDERSTANDING WAVES

- There are two types of **wave**: **longitudinal** and **transverse**.
- A longitudinal wave, like **sound**, has vibrations parallel to the direction of the wave velocity. A transverse wave has vibrations 90 degrees to the direction of the wave velocity.
- **Electromagnetic waves** are transverse waves.
- The **frequency** of a wave is the number of waves produced per unit of time.
- The **wavelength** of a wave is the distance between two neighbouring peaks.
- The speed (v) of the wave in metres per second (m/s) is related to its frequency (f) in hertz (Hz) and the wavelength (λ) in metres (m) by the equation: $v = f\lambda$.

Now try this

a Circle the correct answer.

The speed of a wave is measured in:

    m   m/s   Hz

Wavelength and amplitude can be measured in:

    m   m/s   Hz

Frequency is measured in:

    m   m/s   Hz

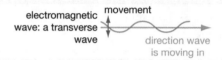

electromagnetic wave: a transverse wave — movement — direction wave is moving in

Homework

1. Draw labelled diagrams to illustrate longitudinal and transverse waves.
2. Use the Internet to research and make a list of transverse waves other than electromagnetic waves.
3. Write a paragraph on the differences and similarities between longitudinal and transverse waves.

ELECTROMAGNETIC WAVES

- **Electromagnetic waves** travel as waves and carry energy from one place to another.
- Electromagnetic waves have different **wavelengths** and **frequencies** but they travel at the same speed of 300 000 kilometres per second in a vacuum.
- The electromagnetic waves in the order of decreasing wavelength (or increasing frequency) are: **radio waves**, **microwaves**, **infrared** (IR), **visible light**, **ultraviolet** (UV), **X-rays** and **gamma rays**.

visible spectrum

longest wavelength					shortest wavelength
radio waves	micro-waves	infrared	ultra-violet	X-rays	gamma rays
lowest frequency					highest frequency

Now try this

b Which of the following statements is/are true?

Statement	True	False
i All electromagnetic waves have the same frequency.	☐	☐
ii Gamma rays have a longer wavelength than radio waves.	☐	☐
iii In a vacuum, radio waves and microwaves have the same speed	☐	☐
iv X-rays are transverse waves.	☐	☐

TOP TIP All electromagnetic waves can be reflected.

Homework

4. Summarise the main properties of electromagnetic waves.
5. Make a list of items in your home that emit electromagnetic waves. For each item, use the information given on page 257 to estimate the wavelength of the waves.
6. Use the Internet to find the distance of the Earth from the Sun. Use this to calculate the time it takes for light to travel from the Sun to Earth.

USES AND HAZARDS OF ELECTROMAGNETIC WAVES

- Radio waves, microwaves, infrared waves and visible light can be used for **communication**.
- Humans do not absorb radio waves.
- Microwaves can heat human tissues.
- Infrared radiation can burn skin.
- Very intense visible light, for example lasers, can be harmful to the eyes.
- Ultraviolet radiation can cause **sunburn** and **cancer**.
- X-rays are used for **imaging** the human skeleton. X-rays pass through soft tissues but are absorbed by bones.
- Both X-rays and gamma rays can **mutate** cells and cause cancer.
- Higher frequency radiation (for example, gamma rays) is more harmful than low frequency radiation (for example, light).

Now try this

c Circle the radiations that can cause cancer in humans.

radio waves

microwaves

infrared waves

visible light

ultraviolet waves

X-rays

gamma rays

Homework

7 Draw a table to show the uses of electromagnetic waves.

8 Outline the hazards of electromagnetic waves.

9 Make a list of potentially hazardous items in the school laboratory that emit electromagnetic waves.

COMMUNICATIONS

- **Radio waves** create an **alternating current** in an aerial of the same frequency as the radio wave.
- The **ionosphere** reflects radio waves. This helps long distance communication.
- Microwaves can pass through the Earth's atmosphere and are used for sending information between the Earth and **satellites**. They are used within mobile phone networks.
- **Infrared waves** and **visible light** can be used to send signals along **optical fibres** and so travel curved paths.
- Modern telecommunications systems use optical fibres to transmit data at high speed over very long distances.
- Communication signals may be **analogue** (continuously varying signals) or **digital** (only two values are possible).
- Digital signals are less prone to **interference** than analogue and are processed by computers.

Now try this

d Circle the electromagnetic waves that can be used for communications.

radio waves

microwaves

infrared waves

visible light

ultraviolet waves

X-rays

gamma rays

Homework

10 Draw a labelled diagram to show how optical fibres reflect light.

11 Explain what is meant by digital signals. Make a list of items in your home that use digital signals.

12 Draw a labelled diagram to show how radio waves can be used for both long-distance communications and for satellite communications.

Radioactivity

ALPHA, BETA AND GAMMA

- An **atom** has a small central **nucleus**, containing **protons** and **neutrons**, which is surrounded by **electrons**.
- Protons have a positive charge, neutrons have no charge and electrons have a negative charge.
- The protons and neutrons are also known as the **nucleons**.
- The nucleus of an atom may be represented as $^A_Z X$, where X is the **chemical symbol**, A is the nucleon or **mass number** and Z is the proton or **atomic number**.
- The **isotopes** of an element are nuclei that have the same number of protons but a different number of neutrons. For example: $^3_2 He$ and $^4_2 He$.
- **Radioactivity** is to do with unstable nuclei.
- The nucleus of a **radioactive** atom emits either an **alpha** (α) particle or a **beta** (β) particle and/or **gamma** (γ) rays.

- All three radiations cause **ionisation**. This means that they can all strip off electrons when colliding with atoms.
- An alpha particle is a slow-moving **helium nucleus** (He). It is a good ioniser and has poor penetrating power. It can be stopped by a thin piece of paper.
- A beta particle is a fast-moving electron. It is a weak ioniser and can be stopped by a few millimetres of aluminium.
- Gamma rays are short-wavelength electromagnetic waves. They are very poor ionisers because they have no charge. They can be stopped by a few centimetres of lead.

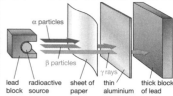

α particles
β particles
γ rays
lead block | radioactive source | sheet of paper | thin aluminium sheet | thick block of lead

Homework

1 Write a paragraph on radioactive nuclei.
2 Draw mind maps for alpha particles, beta particles and gamma rays.

HALF-LIFE

- **Background radiation** is always present and is due to **radioactive** substances in rocks, soil and air, and **cosmic rays**.
- Some background radiation comes from man-made sources, from the nuclear industry and hospital waste.
- The **half-life** of a **radioactive isotope** is the average time taken for half the active nuclei to **decay** or disintegrate.
- After one half-life, the **activity** of the **source** or the **count rate** measured from the source will halve.
- The fraction of nuclei left after one half-life is half, after two half-lives is a quarter, after three half-lives is one-eighth and so on.

Now try this

a Which of the following statements is/are correct?

i   All isotopes have the same half-life. ☐

ii A source containing isotopes of very short half-life will be very active. ☐

iii After one half-life, half of the nuclei have decayed. ☐

iv After two half-lives, a third of the active nuclei will be left. ☐

Homework

3 Use the Internet to find some radioactive isotopes and their half-lives.
4 In your own words explain why a source will have a high activity if there are lots of nuclei and the half-life is very short.

USE OF NUCLEAR RADIATIONS

- **Radioisotopes** are used as **tracers** in industry and hospitals.
- **Gamma** ray emitting tracers are used to find leaks or blockages in underground pipes.
- In medicine, the function of some vital organs can be diagnosed using a radioactive tracer.
- Gamma rays are used to sterilise bandages, syringes and other hospital instruments.
- Irradiating fresh fruit with gamma rays prolongs their shelf life.
- In **radiotherapy**, several gamma ray sources are directed towards cancerous tissues to destroy the cancer cells.
- Domestic smoke detectors contain an **alpha emitting source** (americium).
- The technique of **carbon dating** can be used to date bone, cloth, wood and paper.

 TOP TIP In a paper mill, a beta source can be used to monitor the thickness of the paper.

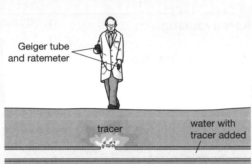

Geiger tube and ratemeter

tracer

water with tracer added

Now try this

b Complete the sentences by filling in the missing words.

Leaks in pipes can be detected using a _____. A radioactive substance emitting gamma rays is put into the pipe. A gamma-emitting source is used because gamma rays can _____ through the pipe and soil. An _____ in the activity above the ground locates the leaks.

Homework

5   Tracers are used in industry and in hospital. Make a list of all the applications.

6   Use the information in the student book (page 269) to explain in your own words how a smoke detector works.

7   Describe how a smoke detector works.

SAFETY ISSUES

- All **ionising** radiations (alpha particles, beta particles and gamma rays) are dangerous.
- All ionising radiations can destroy healthy cells. They can also damage the DNA, leading to **mutation** of cells and cancer.

Now try this

c Find the following key words in this wordsearch.

cancer
cells
alpha
beta
gamma
mutate

R	K	B	N	E	E	T	U
R	A	E	T	I	N	M	O
E	V	T	P	O	U	L	G
C	A	A	G	T	S	R	F
N	L	T	A	L	P	H	A
A	G	T	E	E	N	Y	S
C	E	L	L	S	T	L	E
C	G	G	A	M	M	A	E

Homework

8   Describe how radiation workers protect themselves.

9   Make a list of the precautions you can take to minimise the dangers of using radioactive sources in the laboratory.

10   Make a list of places where you might be exposed to ionising radiation.

The Universe

OBSERVING SPACE AND GRAVITY

- Scientists use Earth-based **telescopes** and observations made from **space probes** (for example, Hubble) to observe the **planets**, **stars** and **galaxies**.
- **Optical telescopes** make use of light to form images. They can be made either from curved mirrors or lenses.
- **Radio telescopes** use radio waves to map out the sky.
- Astronomers also use **gamma rays**, **X-rays**, **ultraviolet radiation** and **infrared radiation** to make observations.
- Observations from the Earth's surface suffer from absorption of electromagnetic waves by its atmosphere. The best location for telescopes is at the top of mountains.
- The **Solar System** has been explored using both manned and unmanned spacecraft.
- All objects, for example planets, moons and stars, exert a **gravitational force**.
- **Gravity** is an attractive force.
- Gravitational force between planets and the Sun keeps planets in **orbit**.

Now try this

a Which of the following statements are true? Place a tick (✓) in the correct column.

Statement	True	False
i Telescopes in space (Hubble) produce good quality images.	☐	☐
ii Radio telescopes use visible light to produce images.	☐	☐
iii Gravity is a repulsive force.	☐	☐
iv The force of gravity holds the Solar System together.	☐	☐

 TOP TIP The gravitational force is larger for massive objects and it gets smaller for longer distances.

Homework

1 Discuss the advantages and disadvantages of having telescopes such as Hubble in space.
2 Use a search engine to look at images produced by Hubble telescope. Make a list of some of these images for the class.
3 Make a list of objects that exert a large gravitational force.

SOLAR SYSTEM

- Our **Sun** and the **Solar System** were formed from a huge mass of gas and dust particles.
- The planets in the order of increasing distance from the Sun are: Mercury, Venus, Earth, Mars, Jupiter, Saturn, Uranus, Neptune and Pluto.
- The rocky planets are: Mercury, Venus, Earth and Mars.
- The gas giants are: Jupiter, Uranus and Neptune.
- Our Moon was created by the collision of the Earth with another small planet during the formation of the Solar System.

Now try this

b Arrange the following in the order of increasing distance from the Earth:

Pluto   Moon   Mars   Sun

Homework

4 Make a mnemonic to remember the order of the planets from the Sun.
5 Use the Internet to obtain some interesting facts about your favourite planet.
6 Make a list of the differences between Mercury and Jupiter.

LIFE AND DEATH OF STARS

- All **stars** are formed from interstellar dust and gas (hydrogen) clouds.
- **Gravitational forces** pull the gases and dust particles together, this is known as **gravitational collapse**. This increases the temperature.
- **Thermonuclear fusion** reactions between hydrogen nuclei start when the temperatures become too high.
- These nuclear reactions release energy in the form of heat and light. A star is born.
- A medium-mass star like our Sun will become a **red giant** and then a **planetary nebula** and a **white dwarf**.
- A heavy-mass star will become a red giant and then a **supernova** and either a **neutron star** or a **black hole**.
- A **black hole** is very dense and has a strong gravitational field from which even light cannot escape.

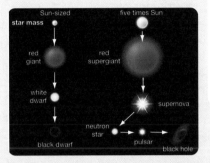

Now try this

c A star is close to its death. Arrange the following stages in the correct sequence for a star like our Sun.

- [ ] red giant
- [ ] star
- [ ] planetary nebula
- [ ] white dwarf

Homework

7 Use the information on page 285 of your student book to describe nuclear fusion.

8 Draw a mind map to show the end of a star like our Sun and one that is much more massive.

9 Research and write a few sentences about red giants, supernovas and black holes.

THE EXPANDING UNIVERSE

- A **galaxy** is a cluster of stars.
- The **Universe** began from a sudden expansion of space some 15 billion years ago. This event is known as the **Big Bang**.
- The evidence that the Universe is expanding comes from the observation that all galaxies are moving away from each other.
- The early Universe was dense and very hot. Its **expansion** led to cooling. The temperature of the Universe is currently −270 °C.
- If a wave source (for example, a galaxy) is moving relative to an observer, then there will be a change in the observed **wavelength** or **frequency**. This is known as the **Doppler effect**.
- The spectrum of light from all galaxies moving away from us shows **red shift** (the entire spectrum is moved to longer wavelengths).
- The further away galaxies are, the greater their speed is and hence red shift is seen.
- If there is not enough matter in the Universe, it will expand forever.
- If there is enough matter in the Universe, gravity will slow down the expansion rate and eventually start to **contract** the Universe towards a **Big Crunch**.

Now try this

d Circle the items that provide evidence of the Big Bang.

red shift

red giants

planets

space is at −270 °C

galaxies are moving away from us

black holes

Homework

10 Discuss all the evidence that points to the creation of the universe.

11 Draw a labelled diagram to illustrate what is meant by red shift.

12 Describe how the fate of the Universe depends on the amount of matter.

Cell activity

CELLS

- The **cell** is the basic unit or 'building block' of all living things.
- Most plant and animal cells contain the following parts:
  - **nucleus**, which controls the activities of the cell and contains the genes.
  - **cytoplasm**, a jelly-like substance where most chemical reactions take place.
  - **cell membrane** to control which substances enter and leave the cell.
  - **mitochondria**, where energy is released in **respiration**.
  - **ribosomes**, where proteins, including enzymes, are made.
- Plant cells may also contain:
  - **chloroplasts**, which absorb light energy for **photosynthesis**.
  - a **cell wall** to strengthen the cell.
  - a large **vacuole** containing cell sap.

Now Try This

a Match the following words to their descriptions.

i Where most chemical reactions take place.	nucleus
ii Where photosynthesis takes place.	cell membrane
iii Where respiration occurs.	cytoplasm
iv Controls the cell's activities.	ribosomes
v Where protein synthesis occurs.	chloroplasts
vi Controls what enters and leaves the cell.	mitochondria

 TOP TIP Cells may be specialised for a particular function, for example sperm cells have a tail to help them 'swim' to the egg.

Homework

1. Which parts are found in plant cells but not animal cells?
2. Draw a labelled diagram of a specialised plant cell.
3. Draw a labelled diagram of a specialised animal cell.

DIFFUSION

- Substances enter or leave cells by **diffusion**.
- Diffusion is the spreading out of particles in a gas or solution.
- Diffusion results in the **net movement** of particles from a region of high **concentration** to a region of low concentration along a **concentration gradient**.
- Diffusion occurs until particles are evenly spread.
- The higher the temperature, the faster the rate of diffusion.
- The steeper the concentration gradient, the faster the rate of diffusion.

Now Try This

b What do you know about diffusion? Are the following statements true (T) or false (F)?

Diffusion is the movement of cells. _____

Diffusion occurs in solids. _____

Particles move from high to low concentration. _____

Diffusion is faster the colder it is. _____

Gas particles spread out by diffusion. _____

Homework

4. Describe **one** example of where diffusion occurs in humans.
5. Describe **one** example of where diffusion occurs in plants.
6. Explain why temperature affects the rate of diffusion.

OSMOSIS

- **Osmosis** is the movement of water molecules.
- Water molecules will move from a **dilute** (weak) solution to a more **concentrated** (strong) solution.
- Osmosis occurs through a **partially permeable membrane**, which allows the passage of water molecules but not solute molecules.
- Water can enter or leave cells by osmosis through the cell membrane.
- This happens at root hair cells where water moves from the soil into the cell by osmosis.

 TOP TIP A dilute solution contains more water particles than a concentrated solution, so water molecules move down their concentration gradient.

Now Try This

c Are the following examples of diffusion (D) or osmosis (O)?

Oxygen moving from the alveoli into the blood. _____

Water moving from the soil to a root hair cell. _____

Carbon dioxide entering a leaf. _____

Carbon dioxide moving from the blood into the lungs. _____

Water passing between cells in a leaf. _____

Glucose moving from the small intestine into the blood. _____

Homework

7 Define the terms **a)** solute, **b)** solvent and **c)** solution.

8 Explain the difference between diffusion and osmosis.

9 Describe how a plant takes up water from the soil.

ENZYMES

- **Enzymes** are **biological catalysts**. They speed up chemical reactions inside cells.
- Enzymes are **protein molecules** made of long chains of **amino acids**.
- The protein molecule is folded to make a specific 3-D shape that other molecules can fit into. This part is called the **active site**.
- High temperatures and extremes of pH can destroy this shape and **denature** the enzyme so it can no longer function.
- Each enzyme has an **optimum temperature** and **pH** under which it functions best.
- Enzymes are not used up or changed during a reaction.
- Enzymes catalyse processes such as respiration, photosynthesis and digestion.

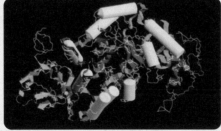

 TOP TIP The molecule an enzyme acts upon is called its substrate. Each enzyme is specific for only one substrate.

Now Try This

d Complete the passage by filling in the missing words.

Enzymes _____ up the rate of chemical reactions. They are _____ molecules which are _____ to produce a 3-D shape. Each enzyme controls just _____ reaction. Enzymes can be _____ by extremes of _____ and _____. Enzymes are not _____ up in chemical reactions.

Homework

10 Explain why heating an enzyme will stop it working.

11 Why will the optimum temperature be different for plant and human enzymes?

12 List **five** examples of enzyme-controlled reactions.

Plant nutrition

PHOTOSYNTHESIS

- Plants make their food, using light energy, by **photosynthesis**.
- The equation for photosynthesis is:
  water + carbon (+ light energy) ⇌ glucose + oxygen
      dioxide
- Water is absorbed by the roots.
- Carbon dioxide enters the leaves via pores called **stomata**.
- Light energy is absorbed by the green pigment **chlorophyll** in the **chloroplasts**.
- This energy is used to combine water and carbon dioxide into **glucose** (sugar).
- Glucose is either respired to release energy or stored as **starch**.
- **Oxygen** is produced as a waste product.

Now Try This

a Match up the following to make correct sentences about photosynthesis.

Oxygen…	**i** …absorbs sunlight energy.
Carbon dioxide…	**ii** …is used in respiration or stored as starch.
Water…	**iii** …enters through the leaves.
Chlorophyll…	**iv** …contain the green pigment chlorophyll.
Glucose…	**v** …is a waste product.
Chloroplasts….	**vi** …enters through the roots.

Homework

1 Why must glucose be converted to starch for storage?
2 Explain why a plant will die if it is kept in the dark for too long.
3 Describe how the raw materials for photosynthesis enter the plant.

SPECIALISED PLANT CELLS

- Water enters the plant via the roots.
- **Root hair cells** are specialised cells that are elongated to provide a greater surface area for absorption of water and minerals.
- Light energy is absorbed by the leaves.
- **Palisade cells** in the upper surface of the leaf are tightly packed together and contain many chloroplasts for absorbing light.
- Carbon dioxide enters through the underside of the leaf.
- Specialised **guard cells** control the opening and closing of the stomata to allow carbon dioxide in and to minimise water loss.

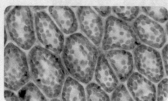

Now Try This

b Match the statements on the left-hand side with the specialised cells.

Contains many chloroplasts.	**i** root hair cell
Found in the lower surface of the leaf.	
Absorbs sunlight energy.	
Contains no chloroplasts.	**ii** palisade cell
Opens and closes the stomata.	
Found in the upper surface of the leaf.	
Has a large surface area.	**iii** guard cell

Homework

4 Explain why not all plant cells contain chloroplasts.
5 Describe the functions of the stomata.
6 Draw a labelled diagram of a root hair cell or a palisade cell.

LIMITING FACTORS

- **Light intensity**, **carbon dioxide** concentration and **temperature** can all affect the rate of photosynthesis.
- Carbon dioxide is a raw material so increasing its availability will mean photosynthesis can occur more rapidly.
- Temperature affects the rate of photosynthesis because it is an enzyme-controlled reaction.
- Increasing the temperature up to the optimum increases the rate of photosynthesis.
- Increasing the temperature above the optimum will **denature** the enzymes, stopping photosynthesis altogether.
- Light intensity provides the energy for the chemical reaction, so increasing light energy will allow a faster rate of reaction.

 TOP TIP Only one factor can limit the rate of photosynthesis at any one time. This will be the factor that is in shortest supply.

Now Try This

c Which is the most likely limiting factor in each case?

A garden plant in the winter _____

Seedlings in a greenhouse during the day _____

A houseplant kept in the shade _____

Algae growing on a pond surface _____

Homework

7   Explain how increasing temperature affects the rate of photosynthesis.

8   Explain how increasing light intensity affects the rate of photosynthesis.

9   Explain how increasing carbon dioxide concentration affects the rate of photosynthesis.

MINERALS

- **Minerals** absorbed in solution by the roots are needed for healthy plant growth.
- **Nitrates** are required for making amino acids, which form proteins.
- Nitrate deficiency will lead to stunted growth.
- **Magnesium** is required to produce chlorophyll.
- Magnesium deficiency will cause yellow leaves.
- **Potassium** and **phosphates** are required for photosynthesis and respiration.
- Lack of potassium causes yellow leaves with dead spots.
- Lack of phosphates leads to poor root growth and purple leaves.

 TOP TIP Farmers and gardeners may add minerals to the soil in order to improve plant growth.

Now Try This

d Complete the passage by filling in the missing words.

Plants need _____ for healthy growth. These are absorbed in _____ through the _____. Nitrates are needed to make _____. _____ is needed to make _____. If plants do not get the minerals they need they will show _____ symptoms. Plants lacking nitrates will show _____ growth. Plants lacking magnesium will have _____ leaves.

Homework

10   Look at **two** different fertiliser packets and list the elements present.

11   Explain why a lack of nitrates will lead to stunted growth.

12   Explain why a lack of magnesium will cause yellow leaves.

Energy and matter

FOOD CHAINS

- Feeding relationships within communities can be represented using **food chains**.
- Light energy from the sun is the source of energy for most food chains.
- Plants are known as **producers** as they capture light energy and convert it into food, which is stored in their cells.
- Animals are called **consumers** because they get their food by eating other organisms.
- **Herbivores** are consumers that only eat plants.
- **Carnivores** eat only meat and omnivores eat both plants and meat.
- A food chain can be summarised as follows:
  producer → primary consumer → secondary consumer → tertiary consumer

Homework

1. Why are green plants known as producers?
2. Make up a food chain containing **four** organisms.
3. Are food chains an accurate way of representing feeding relationships? Explain your answer.

PYRAMIDS OF BIOMASS

- **Biomass** is the mass of living material.
- The biomass at each **trophic level** of a food chain can be drawn to scale and shown as a **pyramid of biomass**.
- The pyramid shows that the biomass decreases as you move along a food chain.
- Pyramids of biomass are more useful than pyramids of numbers because they take into account:
  - the number of organisms at each trophic level.
  - the mass of each organism.
- For example, a single oak tree would be represented as just a single organism in a pyramid of number, giving a 'top heavy' pyramid.
- A pyramid of biomass takes into account the very large mass of the oak tree.

 TOP TIP Biomass, or 'dry' mass, must be used since an organism's mass can change considerably depending on how much water it contains.

Homework

4. Sketch **a)** a pyramid of numbers and **b)** a pyramid of biomass for the following food chain:
   oak tree → caterpillar → bluetit.
5. Why is it more useful to draw a pyramid of biomass than a pyramid of numbers?
6. Why is biomass lost at each stage of a food chain?

ENERGY TRANSFER

- **Energy** and biomass are lost at each trophic level of a food chain:
  - in an organism's waste.
  - through an organism's activities, such as movement.
  - to the surroundings as heat.
- Energy loss through heat is greater in animals that maintain a constant body temperature higher than that of their surroundings, such as mammals and birds.
- The **efficiency** of **food production** can be increased by:
  - reducing the number of stages in food chains.
  - limiting an animal's movement.
  - controlling the temperature of its surroundings.
- Many people find these methods of rearing animals cruel and unacceptable.

 TOP TIP Only about 10 per cent of energy is passed on from one trophic level to the next.

Now Try This

c Complete the passage by filling in the missing words.

Energy is _____ at each stage in a food chain. Some energy is lost in an animal's _____. Some energy is lost due to an animal's _____ and some is lost as _____ to the surroundings. The efficiency of rearing animals can be increased by _____ an animal's movement and controlling the _____ of their surroundings, so less energy is lost through _____ and _____.

Homework

7 What happens to the amount of energy as you move up a food chain? Why?

8 Explain why animals are sometimes reared intensively.

9 Write a paragraph to explain your views on intensive animal rearing.

THE CARBON CYCLE

- Compounds containing **carbon** make up all the tissues of living organisms.
- The amount of **carbon dioxide** in the atmosphere is kept balanced by the **carbon cycle**.
- Plants remove carbon dioxide from the atmosphere by **photosynthesis**.
- Some of this carbon is used in plant growth.
- Carbon dioxide is returned to the atmosphere when plants respire.
- Animals eat the plants and incorporate the carbon into their own tissues.
- Some carbon dioxide is returned to the atmosphere when animals respire.
- **Decomposers** feed on the remains of dead plants and animals and release carbon dioxide from their own respiration.

Now Try This

d How much do you know about the carbon cycle? Are the following statements true (T) or false (F)?

Carbon is found in all living things. _____

Photosynthesis releases carbon dioxide. _____

Plants take in carbon dioxide by respiration. _____

Decomposers release carbon dioxide into the atmosphere. _____

Animals must eat plants to get their carbon. _____

Animals release carbon dioxide into the atmosphere. _____

Homework

10 Explain the role of photosynthesis in the carbon cycle.

11 Explain the role of respiration in the carbon cycle.

12 Explain how burning fossil fuels might upset the balance of the carbon cycle.

Food and energy

THE DIGESTIVE SYSTEM

- **Digestion** is the breakdown of large, insoluble food molecules into smaller, soluble food molecules which can be absorbed.
- In the mouth, the teeth break food into smaller pieces for swallowing and digestion of **starch** begins.
- Food is squeezed down the oesophagus by **peristalsis** before it enters the stomach.
- The stomach contains **hydrochloric acid**, which kills any bacteria that may be present in the food.
- Digestion of **proteins** begins in the stomach.
- Digestion is completed in the **small intestine** and the products are absorbed into the bloodstream.
- The **large intestine** absorbs any excess water from the remaining waste.

Now Try This

a Match the following words with their descriptions.

i	Stores bile.	oesophagus
ii	Excess water is absorbed here.	stomach
iii	Carries food from the mouth to the stomach.	gall bladder
iv	Produces bile.	large intestine
v	Digestion of proteins begins here.	liver

 TOP TIP Each part of the digestive system contains enzymes to break down different food types.

Homework

1 Draw a flowchart to show the passage of food through the digestive system.
2 What is the purpose of the digestive system?
3 Sketch a diagram of the digestive system and label the main organs.

DIGESTIVE ENZYMES

- **Digestive enzymes** catalyse the breakdown of large, insoluble molecules into smaller, soluble molecules.
- **Amylase** is produced in the **salivary glands**, **pancreas** and small intestine.
- Amylase breaks down starch molecules into **glucose** molecules.
- **Protease** is produced in the stomach, pancreas and small intestine.
- Protease breaks down protein molecules into **amino acids**.
- **Lipase** is produced in the pancreas and small intestine.
- Lipase breaks down **lipids** (fats) into **fatty acids** and **glycerol**.
- The liver produces **bile** which neutralises the acidic contents of the stomach as it is emptied into the small intestine.

Now Try This

b Write a part of the digestive system to answer the following.

Where digestion of proteins begins.	_____
Enzymes here will have a low optimum pH.	_____
Enzymes here will have a high optimum pH.	_____
Bile is produced here.	_____
This organ produces all three digestive enzymes.	_____
Hydrochloric acid is produced here.	_____

Homework

4 Make a table to show the enzymes produced in different parts of the digestive system.
5 Explain why the optimum pH of enzymes in the stomach is low.
6 What is the function of bile?

AEROBIC RESPIRATION

- **Aerobic respiration** uses oxygen to release energy from glucose molecules.
- It is an enzyme-catalysed process.
- It takes place in the **mitochondria** of all living cells.
- The equation for aerobic respiration is:
  glucose + oxygen → carbon dioxide + water
- In animals, oxygen for respiration is inhaled and carbon dioxide is exhaled.
- The energy released is used for:
  - building larger molecules from smaller ones.
  - muscle contraction to allow movement in animals.
  - maintenance of a constant body temperature.

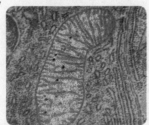

 TOP TIP The equation for aerobic respiration is simply the reverse of the equation for photosynthesis.

Now Try This

c Complete the passage by filling in the missing words.

_____ respiration is the process of releasing _____ from _____ molecules. This requires _____ which is obtained by _____. Respiration occurs in the _____ of all living cells. _____ _____ is a waste product of respiration which is removed from the body by _____. The energy released is used in _____ contraction and maintenance of _____ _____.

Homework

7   Explain why a plant must carry out both photosynthesis and respiration.

8   How is the energy released from respiration used **a)** in animals and **b)** in plants?

9   How are the products of respiration removed from the body?

USES OF ENZYMES

- **Microorganisms** produce enzymes which can be used at home and in industry.
- **Biological** washing powders may contain proteases and lipases to digest and remove food stains.
- Proteases are used to pre-digest protein in baby foods to make it easier to digest.
- **Carbohydrases** are used to make soft-centre chocolates as they break down starch into sugar syrup.
- **Isomerase** is used in slimming products to convert glucose into **fructose**.
- Fructose is much sweeter and can be used in smaller quantities.
- Proteases may also be used to tenderise meat and remove hairs from the skin.

 TOP TIP Enzymes are cheap to use in industry as they work at low temperatures and can be reused.

Now Try This

d How much do you know about enzymes? Are the following statements true (T) or false (F)?

Enzymes are denatured by very low temperatures. _____

Enzymes work slowly at very high temperatures. _____

Enzymes can be reused. _____

Enzymes work best at pH 7. _____

Some enzymes work best under acid conditions. _____

Different enzymes have different optimum conditions. _____

One enzyme may work on many substrates. _____

Homework

10   Why must biological washing powders not be used at high temperatures?

11   List **two** advantages of using enzymes in industry.

12   Explain why enzymes can be reused.

Homeostasis

WASTE REMOVAL

- Humans need to keep the internal environment within their bodies relatively constant. This is called **homeostasis**.
- Conditions such as **temperature**, **pH**, **water** and **blood sugar levels** all affect the activity of cells in the body.
- Waste products such as **carbon dioxide** and **urea** must be removed.
- Carbon dioxide is a waste product of respiration.
- Most carbon dioxide is removed via the lungs when we exhale.
- Urea is produced in the **liver** when excess amino acids are broken down.
- Urea is removed by the **kidneys** and passes out of the body in the **urine**.

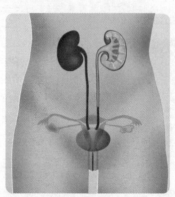

Now Try This

a Link the part(s) of the body to the internal condition(s) it controls.

lungs	**i** blood glucose
kidneys	**ii** carbon dioxide
	iii urea
pancreas	**iv** water content
skin	**v** temperature
	vi pH
liver	**vii** ions

 TOP TIP Urine produced by the kidneys is stored by the bladder before it is released.

Homework

1 Explain what homeostasis means.

2 Why must the water and ion content of the body be kept constant?

3 Why must the body's internal conditions be kept constant?

SKIN AND TEMPERATURE

- The **thermoregulatory centre** in the brain monitors the temperature of the blood flowing through it.
- **Temperature receptors** in the skin also send nervous signals to the brain.
- If the body temperature is too high:
  - **capillaries** in the skin **dilate** (get wider) so more blood flows to the surface and heat is lost.
  - **sweat** is produced, which uses heat from the body to evaporate.
- If the body temperature is too low:
  - capillaries in the skin **constrict** so less blood flows to the surface and less heat is lost.
  - **shivering** occurs so that muscles contract involuntarily. Respiration of the muscle cells produces heat.
- Core body temperature for humans is 37 °C.

Now Try This

b Write 'too hot' or 'too cold' to describe how the body feels when the following happen.

Surface blood vessels become narrower	_____
Less blood flows to surface	_____
Skin looks redder	_____
Sweat glands active	_____
Heat lost by evaporation	_____
Sweat glands inactive	_____

Homework

4 Explain why it is important to maintain a constant body temperature.

5 Describe the changes that occur when body temperature increases.

6 Describe the changes that occur when body temperature decreases.

WATER CONTENT

- The amount of water and **ions** (salts) within the body must be kept relatively constant.
- If there is too much water or too few ions, the body fluids will be too **dilute**.
- Water will enter cells by **osmosis** causing them to swell and burst.
- If there is too little water or too many ions, the body fluids will be too **concentrated**.
- Water will leave cells by osmosis causing them to shrink and be damaged.
- Water is lost from the body in sweat and urine.
- More water is lost through sweating when it is hot. This must be replaced by drinking and eating.
- If there is too little water in the body, less water will be lost in the urine.

Now Try This

c Complete the passage by filling in the missing words.

The concentration of fluids in the body is affected by the amount of _____ and _____. If there is too little water, the body fluids will be too _____. This may cause _____ to be lost from cells by _____ causing them to _____. If there is too much water the body fluids will be too _____. Water will _____ cells by _____ causing them to _____ and _____.

Homework

7 Explain why athletes drink sports drinks rather than water.

8 Describe **two** situations that would increase water loss from the body.

9 How can drinking too little water damage the body?

BLOOD SUGAR

- Blood **glucose** concentration is monitored and controlled by the **pancreas**.
- If blood sugar level is high, the pancreas secretes the hormone **insulin**.
- Insulin causes the **liver** to remove glucose from the blood and store it as **glycogen**.
- If blood sugar level is too low, the pancreas secretes the hormone **glucagon**.
- Glucagon causes the liver to break glycogen down into glucose and release it back into the bloodstream.
- **Diabetes** is a disease where a person's pancreas does not secrete enough insulin.
- Their blood sugar concentration may rise to a fatally high level.
- Diabetes may be treated by insulin injections or a carefully controlled diet.

 TOP TIP Take care with the spelling of the words glycogen and glucagon.

Now Try This

d Match the following words to their descriptions.

i	Acts as a store of glucose in the liver.	pancreas
ii	Hormone that increases blood sugar levels.	liver
iii	Organ which produces insulin.	insulin
iv	A chemical messenger.	glucagon
v	Sugar that is used in respiration.	hormone
vi	Hormone that reduces blood sugar levels.	glycogen
vii	The target organ of insulin and glucagon.	glucose

Homework

10 Use the Internet to research and write a paragraph on diabetes.

11 Describe what happens to blood glucose levels after a meal.

12 Describe what happens to blood glucose levels after exercise.

Inheritance

GENES AND CHROMOSOMES

- Genetic information is found in the **nucleus** of cells.
- **Chromosomes** are made up of large molecules of **DNA** (deoxyribonucleic acid).
- A **gene** is a small section of DNA that controls a particular **characteristic**.
- Each gene codes for a sequence of **amino acids** which makes a particular **protein**.
- Different genes produce different proteins, which cause physical differences in an organism.
- Each person's DNA is unique to them. This can be used to identify individuals by **DNA fingerprinting**.
- In most body cells, chromosomes are found in **homologous pairs**.
- Body cells containing two sets of genetic information are called **diploid** ($2n$).
- **Gametes** are **haploid** (n) meaning there is just one copy of each chromosome.

Now Try This

a Put the following in order of size, starting with the smallest.

- **i** cell
- **ii** gene
- **iii** chromosome
- **iv** nucleus
- **v** DNA molecule
- **vi** organism

TOP TIP The letter n is used to represent the number of different chromosomes.

Homework

1 Explain how genes 'code' for physical characteristics.
2 Explain what the terms **a)** haploid and **b)** diploid mean.
3 Why must gametes be haploid?

MITOSIS AND MEIOSIS

- Body cells divide by **mitosis**.
- During mitosis, the chromosomes are copied and the cell divides once to produce two **daughter cells**.
- Cells produced by mitosis are genetically identical.
- Cell division by mitosis is used for **growth**, **repair** and **asexual reproduction**.
- Cells in the **ovaries** and **testes** divide by **meiosis** to form gametes.
- During meiosis, the chromosomes are copied and the cell divides twice to form four **gametes**.
- Each gamete contains just a single set of chromosomes.
- At **fertilisation**, two gametes fuse to produce a new cell with two sets of chromosomes.

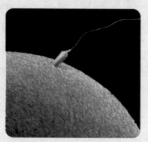

Now Try This

b Write mitosis or meiosis to answer the following questions.

Basis of asexual reproduction	_____
Cells divide once	_____
Produces four daughter cells	_____
Cells divide twice	_____
Produces two daughter cells	_____
Daughter cells are haploid	_____

TOP TIP At fertilisation, two haploid gametes join to form a diploid zygote: $n + n = 2n$

Homework

4 Explain why a baby may resemble both parents.
5 Why do populations of asexually reproduced organisms show little variation?
6 Explain how sexual reproduction leads to variation.

INHERITANCE

- In humans, chromosome 23 carries the genes that determine **gender**.
- In females, the **sex chromosomes** are the same (XX) and in males they are different (XY).
- All egg cells carry the **X chromosome**; sperm cells carry either an X or Y.
- Some **characteristics** are controlled by a single **gene**.
- Genes have different forms called **alleles**, for example the gene for eye colour may have alleles for blue, brown or green eyes.
- Organisms **inherit** two alleles for each characteristic – one from the mother and one from the father.
- Only a single copy of a **dominant** allele is required for it to be expressed.
- In order for a **recessive** allele to be expressed, both copies of a gene must be recessive.

Now Try This

c Match the following words to their descriptions.

i Alternative forms of a gene.   dominant

ii When both forms of a gene are the same.   gene

iii Only one copy of this type of gene is needed to be expressed.   homozygous

iv When two alleles of the same gene are different.   heterozygous

v A small section of DNA.   alleles

 TOP TIP Dominant alleles are represented with a capital letter, recessive alleles with a lower case letter.

Homework

7 Draw a genetic diagram of a cross between two brown eyed individuals (Bb).

8 Explain the difference between a gene and an allele.

9 Explain the difference between a dominant and a recessive allele.

GENETIC DISORDERS

- Some **disorders** are caused by faulty genes and can be **inherited**.
- **Cystic fibrosis** (CF) affects cell membranes causing thick, sticky mucus in the lungs and gut.

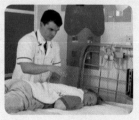

- Cystic fibrosis is caused by a **recessive allele**.
- Two **heterozygous** parents have a one in four chance of passing it on to their offspring.
- **Huntingdon's disease** affects the nervous system causing tremors, writhing and dementia.
- Huntingdon's disease is caused by a **dominant allele**, so can be passed on by just one parent.
- A parent with Huntingdon's has a one in two chance of passing on the allele.

Now Try This

d Complete the passage by filling in the missing words.

Some disorders are caused by a _____ gene and can be _____. For example, _____ _____ is a disorder of cell membranes. It is caused by a _____ _____ allele. Heterozygous individuals are called _____. Two carriers have a one in _____ chance of passing on the disorder. Huntingdon's disease is caused by a _____ allele. A person with the Huntingdon's allele has a one in _____ chance of passing it on to their offspring.

Homework

10 Draw a genetic diagram to illustrate a cross between two carriers of CF.

11 Draw a genetic diagram to show a cross between a Huntingdon's sufferer and a healthy individual.

12 Explain what is meant by a 'carrier' of cystic fibrosis.

Looking more closely at the atom

STRUCTURE OF THE ATOM

- Atoms have a central **nucleus** made of **protons** and **neutrons**.
- Around the central nucleus are **electrons**.
- Protons have a charge of +1; electrons have a charge of −1; neutrons are neutral (a charge of 0).
- Atoms always have the same number of protons as electrons. This is why they are always neutral.
- The number of protons an atom has is called its **atomic (proton) number**.

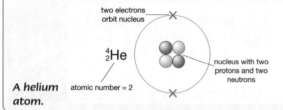

two electrons orbit nucleus

$_{2}^{4}\text{He}$

atomic number = 2

nucleus with two protons and two neutrons

A helium atom.

Now try this

a Circle the correct answer.

  i Protons have the same **size** charge as

    atoms   neutrons   electrons

  ii Electrons have a charge of

    +1   −1   0

  iii Electrons orbit the

    nucleus   shells   molecule

  iv The atomic number is the number of

    protons   atoms   neutrons

  v The nucleus contains

    electrons   atoms   protons + neutrons

Homework

1 Explain why atoms are neutral.

2 Find the proton numbers of the following atoms: carbon, copper, chromium, calcium.

3 Use the Internet to find out when electrons were first discovered and by whom.

WHERE DO THE ELECTRONS GO?

- **Electrons** occupy particular **energy levels** (or **shells**).
- Electrons always occupy the lowest possible energy level available (the shell closest to the nucleus with a space).
- The lowest energy level can hold up to two electrons. The second holds up to eight and the third up to eight.
- When we arrange the elements in the **periodic table** they are always in order of their **atomic number**.
- Elements in the same group of the periodic table always have the same number of electrons in their highest energy level (outer shell).
- An atom of magnesium can be shown like this:

Now try this

b Use your periodic table to fill in the gaps.

The atomic number of calcium is _____. Calcium atoms have _____ protons and _____ electrons. The electrons in calcium are arranged _____, _____, _____, _____.

> **TOP TIP** The noble gases all have full outer shells of electrons. This is what makes them unreactive.

Homework

4 Draw diagrams to show the electron arrangements of lithium, sodium and potassium.

5 What do these three group 1 metals have in common in terms of their electrons?

6 Guess at the number of outer electrons in iodine.

WHAT HAPPENS WHEN ELEMENTS COMBINE?

- When two or more elements form a **compound** the elements are not just mixed, they cannot be separated from each other and are **chemically combined**.
- **Bonding** involves **electrons** from the highest energy level only (those in the outer shell).
- These electrons can be given away by one atom and taken by another. We say the electrons have been **transferred**.
- When an atom loses an electron it forms a positively charged **ion**.
- When an atom gains an electron it forms a negatively charged ion.
- The ions that form always have the electron structure of their nearest **noble gas** (in group 0).
- The oppositely charged ions attract each other forming a **giant ionic lattice**. This is **ionic bonding**.

Now try this

c Complete the sentences by filling in the missing words.

When sodium and chlorine react together to make the _____ sodium chloride, the sodium atom loses an electron and forms an _____ with a _____ charge. The ion now has the electron structure of _____, its nearest noble gas. The chlorine atom gains the electron and forms an ion with a _____ charge. The chlorine now has the electronic structure of argon, its nearest _____ gas. The oppositely charged ions attract each other forming a giant ionic _____.

Homework

7 Which particle in the atom is involved when atoms combine to form compounds?

8 What is the charge on the ions formed by **a)** lithium **b)** sodium **c)** calcium?

9 What is the charge on the ions formed by **a)** chlorine **b)** oxygen **c)** iodine?

ALKALI METALS AND HALOGENS

- The **elements** in **group 1** of the **periodic table** (the **alkali metals**) behave in a similar way.
- The alkali metals all react with non-metals to form **ionic compounds** in which the **metal ion** has a 1+ charge.
- The ion that forms can be shown like this:

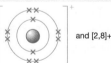

(Na+)   and [2,8]+

- The elements in **group 7**, the **halogens**, all behave in a similar way.
- The halogens react with the alkali metals to form ionic compounds in which the **halide ion** has a 1– charge.

Now try this

d Chlorine atoms have seven electrons in their highest energy level. Sodium atoms have one in theirs. Answer these questions about bromine and rubidium.

How many electrons in the highest energy level of rubidium atoms? _____

What charge do rubidium ions have? _____

What electronic structure does a rubidium ion have? It is like that of _____

How many electrons in the highest energy level of bromine atoms? _____

What charge do bromide ions have? _____

What electronic structure does a bromide ion have? It is like that of _____

Homework

10 What type of bonding will occur when sodium reacts with chlorine?

11 Why do chlorine and bromine behave in a similar way?

12 Use the Internet to find out the meanings of the words chlorine and bromine.

Structure and bonding

WHAT PROPERTIES DO IONIC COMPOUNDS HAVE?

- **Ionic compounds** have regular structures (**ionic lattices**).
- There are strong **electrostatic forces** between the oppositely charged **ions**.
- As these forces are difficult to overcome, ionic compounds have high melting points and boiling points.
- When you dissolve an ionic compound in water or melt it, the ions are free to move.
- When free to move, the ions are able to move and carry an electrical current.

 TOP TIP Ionic compounds do not conduct electricity when solid because the ions cannot move.

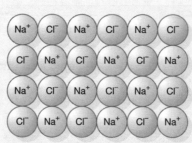

Now try this

a Circle the correct answer.

i Ionic compounds contain

    atoms   ions   molecules

ii Forces holding ions together are

    electrostatic   magnetic

        gravitational

iii Melting points of ionic compounds

    high   low   100 °C

iv Ionic compounds conduct if

    pure   hot   molten

v Electrostatic forces between ions

    impossible   strong   weak

Homework

1 What is meant by the term 'ionic lattice'?

2 Why are ionic substances solids with fairly high melting points?

3 Explain why ionic compounds conduct when molten but not when solid.

COVALENT BONDING AND SIMPLE MOLECULES

- When **non-metals** combine, they share their electrons forming **covalent bonds**.
- Covalent bonds are strong.
- Some covalently bonded substances form simple **molecules**.
- Examples are: H_2, Cl_2, O_2, HCl, H_2O, CH_4.
- There are only weak forces between molecules.
- Simple molecules are solids, liquids or gases with fairly low melting and boiling points.
- Since the molecules have no overall charge, substances made of molecules do not conduct electricity.

Now try this

b In these sentences, cross out the incorrect word in each pair, leaving the correct word.

Covalent bonding involves **transfer/sharing** of electrons to form **complex/simple** molecules. The forces holding the atoms together are **weak/strong** but the forces between molecules are **weak/strong**. Covalent molecules have **high/low** melting and boiling points and they **do/do not** conduct electricity because they are electrically **neutral/charged**.

Homework

4 Give **three** more examples of compounds that must be covalently bonded.

5 Why are many covalent molecules gases or liquids with fairly low melting points?

6 Draw up a table to compare the properties of ionic and covalent compounds.

METALS

- The **electrons** in the highest energy level (outer shell) are **delocalised**.
- This leaves positively charged metal **ions** which have a regular arrangement.
- The structure is held together by the **electrostatic attraction** between the positive ions and negative electrons.
- The delocalised electrons allow the metal to **conduct** heat and electricity.
- Layers of atoms can slide over each other, so metals can be bent and shaped.

 In ionic compounds the ions are the charge carrier. In metals it is the electrons which carry the charge.

Now try this

c Add these labels to the diagram to show a metallic structure.

  i   Regular arrangement of atoms
  ii Outer electrons delocalised
  iii Positive metal ions
  iv Delocalised electrons hold metal ions together

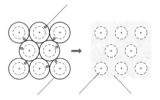

Homework

7 In your own words, explain why all metals except mercury are solids.

8 Explain why metals can be bent or hammered into shape.

9 Explain what is meant by the word 'delocalised'.

GIANT COVALENT SUBSTANCES AND NANOPARTICLES

- **Diamond**, **graphite** (both forms of carbon) and **silicon dioxide** (silica) are **covalently bonded** but form **giant structures** (lattices) or **macromolecules**.
- Each atom in these structures is held by many covalent bonds so these substances have very high melting and boiling points.
- Diamond is very hard because each atom is held by four strong bonds.
- The delocalised electrons in graphite allow graphite to conduct electricity.
- The layers in graphite are only held together weakly and can therefore slip over each other. This makes graphite slippery and soft.
- **Nanoscience** is about particles between 1 and 100 nm in size and made of a few hundred atoms.
- A **nm (nanometre)** is one million times smaller than a millimetre.
- **Nanoparticles** show different properties from the material when it is in bulk form.
- Nanoparticles have a high surface area to volume ratio.
- Nanoparticles may lead to new developments in: computers, catalysts, coatings, stronger and lighter construction materials and very selective sensors.

Homework

10 Explain why graphite conducts electricity but diamond does not.

11 Explain why graphite feels slippery.

12 Find out which giant covalent substance is famous in Keswick, the Lake District.

Mass and moles

MASSES AND MOLES

- The heavy bits of an atom are the **protons** and **neutrons**.

Particle	proton	neutron	electron
Mass	1	1	very small

- The total number of protons plus neutrons is called the **mass number**.
- To find the number of protons, take the **atomic number** from the mass number.
- Not all atoms of an element are identical. Some have different numbers of neutrons and these are called **isotopes**.
- The **relative atomic mass** (A_r) of an element is how heavy the atoms of that element are compared to atoms of **carbon-12**. It takes all isotopes into account.
- Carbon-12 is an atom of carbon which has a mass number of 12.

Now try this

a Match the item in the left-hand column with the number in the right-hand column.

i	A_r of Cl	20
ii	protons in Ca atom	8
iii	neutrons in $^{12}_{6}C$	35.5
iv	atomic number of O	6
v	mass number of C in $^{12}_{6}C$	12

 Don't forget – the number in a formula applies only to the element it follows or, if there are brackets, everything in the brackets.

Homework

1 How many protons, neutrons and electrons are there in **a)** $^{39}_{19}K$ **b)** $^{35}_{17}Cl$ **c)** $^{37}_{17}Cl$?
2 What do we call atoms like those in **b)** and **c)** above?
3 What do you understand by the term 'relative atomic mass'?

FORMULA MASS, THE MOLE AND PERCENTAGE COMPOSITION

- The **relative formula mass** (M_r) of a compound is found by adding together the **relative atomic mass** of all the atoms found in the **formula**.
- $CaCO_3$ has one atom of Ca (40), one atom of C (12) and three atoms of O (3 × 16), so the M_r is 40 + 12 + 48 = 100.
- One **mole** of a substance is the relative mass expressed in grams.
- Percentage of an element in a compound =
$$\frac{\text{relative mass of element}}{\text{relative formula mass}} \times 100\,\%$$

 When finding the percentage mass of an element, remember to find all of the atoms of that element.

Now try this

b Circle the correct answer.

M_r of CO_2	56	44	28
M_r of $Ca(OH)_2$	74	54	114
Mass of one mole of H_2O	18	10	12
Percentage of C in CO_2	44	27	12
Mass of two moles CO_2	112	56	88
Percentage of N in NH_4NO_3	18	35	17

Homework

4 Calculate the M_r of the following: **a)** MgO **b)** $CaCl_2$ **c)** $Mg(OH)_2$ **d)** $(NH_4)_2SO_4$.
5 Calculate the percentage of **a)** Mg in MgO **b)** Cl in $CaCl_2$ **c)** N in $(NH_4)_2SO_4$.
6 What is the mass of **five** moles of CO_2?

REACTING MASSES

- We can find how much **reactant** is needed or how much **product** is made using the **balanced symbol equation** of a reaction.
- If you are asked what mass of MgO is formed when 4.8 g of Mg burns, you must first refer to the equation: $2Mg + O_2 \rightarrow 2MgO$.
- The equation tells us that two **moles** Mg react to make two moles MgO.
- Next work out the mass of two moles Mg. This is $2 \times 24 = 48$ g.
- Then work out the mass of two moles MgO. This is $2 \times (24 + 16) = 80$ g.
- This tells us that 48 g of Mg gives 80 g of MgO.
- 4.8 g of Mg is 10 times less Mg so we will get 10 times less MgO.
- 4.8 g of Mg will give 8.0 g of MgO.

Now try this

c When sodium reacts with water the equation is: $2Na + 2H_2O \rightarrow 2NaOH + H_2$.

What is the mass of one mole of Na? _____

What is the mass of two moles of Na? _____

What is the mass of one mole of H_2? _____

How many moles of NaOH would be made from two moles of Na? _____

What mass of NaOH would be made from 46 g of Na? _____

What mass of H_2 would be made from 4.6 g of Na? _____

Homework

Refer to this equation and answer the following questions: $CaCO_3 + 2HCl \rightarrow CaCl_2 + CO_2 + H_2O$

7 What mass of CO_2 is made when 200 g of $CaCO_3$ is reacted completely?

8 What mass of $CaCO_3$ is needed to make 4.4 g of carbon dioxide?

9 What mass of water is made when 100 kg of calcium carbonate reacts completely?

WE DON'T ALWAYS GET AS MUCH PRODUCT AS WE EXPECT

- No atoms are lost or gained during reactions but some may turn into substances that we are not trying to make.
- Some of the **product** may be lost when trying to separate it from the mixture.
- The **reactants** may not completely convert into products. The **reaction** may not go to completion.
- The amount of product obtained is known as the **yield**.
- **Percentage yield** of a product =
$$\frac{\text{mass product obtained}}{\text{mass that could theoretically be obtained}} \times 100\ \%$$
- Another way of measuring the **efficiency** of a reaction is to calculate its **atom economy**.
$$\text{Atom economy} = \frac{\text{mass of atoms in useful product}}{\text{mass of atoms of reactants}} \times 100\%$$
- It is important to consider atom economy for economical reasons and to increase sustainability.

Now try this

d Complete the sentences by filling in the missing words. Choose from this list:

**economic   product   yields
lost   completion**

Chemists are always interested in achieving high _____ of products. A 100% yield may not be obtained if the reaction does not go to _____ or if some other _____ forms in a different reaction from the intended one. Some product can be _____ when separating it from the reaction mixture. Atom economy is important for _____ reasons.

Homework

10 What do you understand by the term 'yield'?

11 Give **three** reasons why reactions may not give 100 per cent yield.

12 Explain why it is important to consider the atom economy of a reaction.

Rates of reaction

MEASURING RATES OF REACTION

- You can measure how fast a reaction is occurring by measuring the amount of a reactant used up over a period of time or by measuring the amount of a product that has formed over a certain time.

- Rate of reaction = $\dfrac{\text{reactant used up/product formed}}{\text{time taken}}$

- The rate of reaction can be increased in four ways:
  - increase the **temperature**
  - increase the **concentration** of solutions (or **pressure** of reacting gases)
  - increase the **surface area** of solid reactants
  - add a **catalyst**

Now try this

a What effect will each of the following changes have on the rate of reaction between magnesium and hydrochloric acid? Answer using **increase** or **decrease** or **no effect**.

Increasing the concentration of hydrochloric acid. _____

Adding water to the acid. _____

Adding a catalyst. _____

Using powdered magnesium instead of magnesium ribbon. _____

Homework

1 If it takes 120 seconds to make 40 cm³ of gas in a reaction, calculate the rate in cm³/s.

2 Explain how you could measure the rate of reaction when $CaCO_3$ reacts with HCl.

3 Give **three** ways in which you could speed up the reaction between $CaCO_3$ and HCl.

COLLISION THEORY

- **Particles** can only **react** if they **collide** with enough energy.
- The minimum amount of energy a particle must have for a successful reaction is called the **activation energy**.
- Increasing the **temperature** increases the speed of reacting particles, so they collide more frequently and with more energy.
- Increasing the concentration of a solution increases the **frequency of collisions**.
- If two gases are at the same pressure and temperature then equal volumes will contain equal numbers of molecules.
- Increasing the pressure of gases means there are more molecules in the same volume so there will be more frequent collisions.

 TOP TIP Concentrations of solutions are given in mol/dm³. If the concentration is 2 mol/dm³ then there are two moles of solute in 1 dm³ of solution.

Now try this

b Match the changes on the left-hand side to the effect on the right-hand side. You can link each statement to one or both of the effects.

i Increasing the temperature

ii Increasing the pressure of a gas

iii Increasing the surface area of a solid

iv Increasing the concentration of a solution

more frequent collisions

more energetic collisions

Homework

4 Create a poster to illustrate the 'Collision theory'.

5 **a)** Explain what is meant by 'activation energy'.

  b) If you had to explain this term to a Year 7 student, what example would you give to help you?

CATALYSTS

- **Catalysts** speed up the **rate of reaction**.
- Catalysts are not used up during reactions.
- Catalysts are important in industry.
- Catalysts reduce costs in industry because they make reactions happen more quickly.

 Catalysts are often transition metals or their compounds.

Now try this

c Complete the sentences below by filling in the missing words.

Catalysts are very important in industry because they make reactions go _____, which reduces _____. Reactants are used up during reactions but _____ are not. Catalysts are often _____ metals or their compounds.

Homework

6 Use the Internet to make a chart showing different catalysts and the reactions they are used in.

7 In your chart, put a tick by the catalysts that contain transition metals.

8 Explain why catalysts are so useful in industry.

ENERGY CHANGES DURING REACTIONS

- When reactions occur, energy may be given out to the surroundings. These are **exothermic** reactions.
- When an acid **neutralises** an alkali, heat energy is given out. This reaction is exothermic.
- Other exothermic reactions are **oxidation** and **combustion** (burning).
- When reactions occur, energy may be taken in from the surroundings. These are **endothermic** reactions.
- An example of an endothermic reaction is when calcium carbonate is **thermally decomposed** into calcium oxide and carbon dioxide.
- All thermal decompositions are endothermic.
- Some reactions are **reversible**. An example is:

  hydrated copper sulfate ⇌ anhydrous copper sulfate + water
  (blue)   (white)

- If a reaction is reversible and it is endothermic in one direction then it will be exothermic in the other direction.
- The same amount of energy is transferred in either direction in a reversible reaction.

 Water will turn white anhydrous copper sulfate blue.

Now try this

d Answer the following questions using the words **exothermic** or **endothermic**.

A reaction that gives out heat energy. _____

Driving water off hydrated copper sulfate. _____

Combustion reactions. _____

Thermal decomposition reactions. _____

Adding water to anhydrous copper sulfate. _____

A reaction that takes in heat energy. _____

Neutralisations. _____

Homework

9 Find out how the hand warmers used by campers, walkers and fishermen work.

10 Make a poster to illustrate the terms 'exothermic', 'endothermic' and 'activation energy'.

11 Is it true that all combustion reactions are exothermic?

Equilibrium reactions

REVERSIBLE REACTIONS

- In **reversible reactions**, the **reactants** make the **products** but these can turn back into the reactants again. The reaction does not go to **completion**. For example:
  ammonium chloride $\rightleftharpoons$ ammonia + hydrogen chloride.
- Reversible reactions occurring in **closed systems** reach **equilibrium**. A closed system is one into which no chemicals can enter or leave.
- At equilibrium, the reactants are turning into products at the same rate as the products are turning back into reactants.
- The proportion of reactants and products present at equilibrium depends on the conditions, for example, temperature and pressure.
- The Haber process, used to manufacture ammonia, is a reversible reaction.

Now try this

a Complete the sentences by filling in the missing words.

The _____ process involves reacting nitrogen and hydrogen to make ammonia. Nitrogen and hydrogen are the _____ and the product of this reaction is _____. If ammonia is made in a closed system, because it is a _____ reaction, an equilibrium will be reached. By carefully choosing the right _____ and pressure we can make sure the amount of ammonia made is as high as possible.

Homework

1 What factors affect the position of equilibrium?
2 What do you understand by the term 'a closed system'?
3 Describe **two** reactions which are reversible reactions.

THE HABER PROCESS

- The raw materials for the **Haber process** are **hydrogen** and **nitrogen**.
- Nitrogen is obtained from the air and hydrogen from natural gas.
- The gases are first purified, then they are passed over a **catalyst** of iron at a temperature of 450 °C and a pressure of 200 atmospheres.
- The reaction reaches **equilibrium** when hydrogen and nitrogen are combining at the same rate as the ammonia is decomposing.
- The equation for this reaction is: $3H_2 + N_2 \rightleftharpoons 2NH_3$.
- The ammonia can be removed from the mixture by cooling it. Ammonia easily turns into a liquid and can be tapped off.
- The unreacted hydrogen and nitrogen are then recycled by returning them to the reactor.

Now try this

b Circle the correct answers for these questions, which are all about the Haber process. There may be one or two for each question!

i What are the reactants?
   nitrogen   ammonia   hydrogen
ii What does the process make?
   air   methane   ammonia
iii What is the catalyst?
   iron   platinum   nickel
iv What conditions are used?
   200 °C   450 °C   200 atm

Homework

4 Draw a flow chart to show the Haber process.
5 What are the conditions used in the Haber process?
6 Find out who taught Fritz Haber chemistry when he was at university in Berlin.

FACTORS THAT AFFECT THE RATE AND YIELD OF REACTION

- A high temperature always gives a fast rate of reaction.
- A high pressure always gives a fast rate of reaction.
- If a reaction is **exothermic**, then having a high temperature will decrease the **yield**.
- If a reaction is **endothermic**, then having a high temperature will increase the yield.
- In a reaction involving gases, an increase in pressure always pushes the reaction to the side of the equation with the smallest number of gas molecules.
- A **catalyst** speeds up the reaction but does not affect the yield.

Now try this

c Answer the following questions by writing **increase**, **decrease** or **no effect**.

For the reaction $A_{(g)} + B_{(g)} \rightleftharpoons C_{(g)}$ which is endothermic, what would be the effect of:

Increasing temperature on the rate of reaction? _____

Increasing the pressure on the rate of reaction? _____

Using a catalyst on the rate of reaction? _____

Increasing the pressure on the yield of C? _____

Increasing the temperature on the yield of C? _____

Homework

7 Give **three** conditions that are used to speed up reactions.

8 Give **two** conditions that are used to give a high yield in endothermic reactions.

9 How does a catalyst affect the yield of a reaction?

CHOOSING THE CONDITIONS FOR THE HABER PROCESS

- The equation for the **Haber process** is:
  $$3H_{2(g)} + N_{2(g)} \rightleftharpoons 2NH_{3(g)}.$$
- The Haber process is an **exothermic reaction**.
- A high temperature gives a high rate of reaction but a poor yield of **ammonia**.
- A moderate temperature of 450 °C is used to obtain a reasonable yield of ammonia at a reasonable rate. It is a compromise between speed and yield.
- A **catalyst of iron** increases the reaction rate.
- A high pressure gives a fast rate and a high yield.
- A moderately high pressure is used because high pressures need more energy to create them and more expensive equipment to withstand them.
- Conditions chosen allow a good rate of reaction and a fairly good yield but minimise waste energy, which is economically and environmentally important.

d Write **increase**, **decrease** or **no effect** to answer these questions about the Haber process. What is the effect of:

Increasing temperature on rate? _____

Increasing pressure on rate? _____

Using a catalyst on the rate? _____

Increasing temperature on yield? _____

Increasing pressure on yield? _____

Using a catalyst on yield? _____

Using a catalyst on cost? _____

Using lower pressures on safety? _____

Homework

10 Write a word equation for the Haber process.

11 A low temperature gives a good yield of ammonia, so why is a moderate temperature used?

12 A high pressure gives a good rate of reaction, so why is a moderate pressure used?

Ions in solution

ELECTROLYSIS

- **Ionic substances** do not conduct electricity when solid, but do when molten or dissolved in water because the ions can move.
- Positive ions move to the **negative electrode** during **electrolysis** and negative ions move to the **positive electrode**.
- At the negative electrode, ions gain electrons. This is **reduction**. At the positive electrode, ions lose electrons – **oxidation**.
- If there is a mixture of ions, the products formed depend on the reactivity of the elements involved.

 Metal ions are always positive. Non-metal ions are negative.

Now try this

a Add these labels to the diagram to show what happens during electrolysis of molten sodium chloride.

positive electrode   negative electrode
electrons   reduction   oxidation

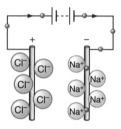

Homework

1 Explain why solid sodium chloride cannot conduct but when dissolved in water it can.

2 During electrolysis of molten lead bromide, where will a) the bromine b) the lead go?

3 Find out what the term REDOX means.

MORE ELECTROLYSIS

- The **half-equations** for the reactions at the **electrodes** during **electrolysis** of molten NaCl are:
$$2Cl^- \rightarrow Cl_2 + 2e^- \qquad Na^+ + e^- \rightarrow Na$$
- When aqueous sodium chloride is electrolysed we get different products because there are ions from the water present as well.
- Electrolysis of $NaCl_{(aq)}$ makes hydrogen at the negative electrode, chlorine at the positive electrode and leaves sodium hydroxide in the solution.
- **Copper** can be **purified** using electrolysis.
- An impure piece of copper is made at the positive electrode. Here Cu is oxidised (electrons are lost) and $Cu^{2+}_{(aq)}$ ions are made. They are attracted to the negative electrode.
- At the negative electrode, the $Cu^{2+}_{(aq)}$ ions gain electrons (are reduced) and deposit pure copper on the negative electrode.
- Unreactive impurities drop to the bottom of the tank and more reactive impurities go into the solution.

Now try this

b Complete the following sentences by filling in the missing word (**reduction** or **oxidation**).

Happens:

when electrons are gained _____

at the negative electrode _____

at the positive electrode _____

when electrons are lost _____

when copper is deposited at the negative electrode _____

Homework

4 During the electrolysis of molten sodium chloride, what forms at the negative electrode?

5 Draw a diagram showing how Mg and Au impurities are removed from Cu by electrolysis.

6 What **three** products form during the electrolysis of salt solution, $NaCl_{(aq)}$?

MAKING SALTS

- **Insoluble salts** can be made by mixing two solutions together so that a **precipitate** forms.
- For example, lead sulfate can be made by mixing together solutions of lead nitrate and sodium sulfate. The solutions contain the ions needed to make the insoluble lead sulfate.
- Precipitation can be used to remove unwanted ions from solutions.
- $Ca^{2+}_{(aq)}$ can be removed from water by adding $CO_3^{2-}_{(aq)}$ ions. A precipitate of $CaCO_{3(s)}$ forms. This removes the hardness from the water.
- Precipitation can also be used to remove unwanted ions from effluent.
- Soluble salts can be made in a number of different ways involving reactions with acids.
- Hydrochloric acid makes salts called **chlorides**, sulfuric acid makes **sulfates** and nitric acid makes **nitrates**.

Salt crystals can be crystallised to make solid salt.

Now try this

c Name the salt formed when the following are mixed.

$Ca^{2+}_{(aq)}$ and $CO_3^{2-}_{(aq)}$

_____

Hydrochloric acid and magnesium

_____

Sulfuric acid and sodium hydroxide

_____

Nitric acid and copper oxide

_____

$Pb^{2+}_{(aq)}$ and $SO_4^{2-}_{(aq)}$

_____

Homework

7 Give **three** uses for precipitation reactions.

8 What salts will form when these acids react: **a)** sulfuric **b)** hydrochloric **c)** nitric **d)** citric?

9 What **two** solutions could be added to make some solid $PbSO_4$?

RADIATION PROPERTIES

- **Soluble salts** can be made by reacting metals with acids. Some metals are too reactive and some do not react.
- If a metal is too reactive the acid can be reacted with a **base** or an **alkali**.
- A base is a **metal oxide** or **hydroxide**. A soluble base is an alkali.
- If an alkali is used, we know when the acid is **neutralised** by using an **indicator**.
- **Ammonia** dissolves in water to make an alkali. When reacted with acids it makes **ammonium salts**, which are used as **fertilisers**.
- If an insoluble base is used, we know when the acid is neutralised because no more base will dissolve.
- $H^+_{(aq)}$ ions make solutions acidic, $OH^-_{(aq)}$ ions make solutions alkaline.
- During **neutralisation** these two ions react to make water: H^+ and OH^-.
- The equation for neutralisation is: $H^+_{(aq)} + OH^-_{(aq)} \rightarrow H_2O_{(l)}$.

Now try this

d Fill in the missing words in these sentences.

If we want to make the fertiliser ammonium nitrate we need to react ammonia, which is an _____, with _____ acid. We need to know when just the right amount of each solution is present and to do this we use an _____. The ammonia contains _____ ions and the acid contains _____ ions and when these ions react with each other they make _____.

Homework

10 Name **two** metals that would be too reactive to add to an acid.

11 Name **two** metals that would be too unreactive to react with acids.

12 Explain in words what this equation tells you: $H^+_{(aq)} + OH^-_{(aq)} \rightarrow H_2O_{(l)}$.

The way things move

SPEED

- The **speed** of an object depends on the distance it covers in a given time.
- The speed of an object is defined as 'the rate of change of distance travelled'.
- For an object travelling at a constant speed, the speed is given by the equation:

$$\text{speed} = \frac{\text{distance}}{\text{time}}$$

- Other helpful equations are: distance = speed × time

$$\text{time} = \frac{\text{distance}}{\text{speed}}$$

- For an object not travelling at constant speed, the **average speed** is given by the equation:

$$\text{average speed} = \frac{\text{total distance travelled}}{\text{total time taken}}$$

- Speed can be measured in metres per second (m/s), kilometres per hour (km/h) and so on.
- An object travelling at a constant speed of 3.0 m/s will travel a distance of 3.0 m in a time of 1.0 s.
- **Velocity** may be defined as the speed in a certain direction.
- For example, a car travels a distance of 70 km in 1.2 hours. Calculate its average speed in km/h and in m/s.

$$\text{average speed} = \frac{\text{distance}}{\text{time}} = \frac{70 \text{ km}}{1.2 \text{ h}} = 58.3 \text{ km/h}$$

$$\text{average speed} = \frac{\text{distance}}{\text{time}} = \frac{70\,000 \text{ m}}{(1.2 \times 3600) \text{ s}} = 16.2 \text{ m/s}$$

Now try this

a Circle the correct answer.

i What is the correct unit for speed?

km   m/s

ii An object has speed 5 km/h. What distance does it travel in 2 hours?

2.5 km   10 km

iii Is it true that doubling the speed will double the distance travelled in a given time?

yes   no

Homework

1 Describe how you would determine your average speed.
2 Use the Internet to find the typical speed of **three** objects (for example, cars). Use this to determine the distance travelled by each object in a time of 10 seconds.
3 Write down some of the similarities and differences between speed and velocity.

ACCELERATION

- An object 'speeding up' has **acceleration**.
- An object 'slowing down' has negative acceleration, or has **deceleration**.
- Acceleration is equal to the rate of change of **velocity**.
- acceleration = $\dfrac{\text{change in velocity}}{\text{time taken}}$
- Acceleration is measured in m/s^2.
- Uniform acceleration means an object with a constant acceleration.
- An object moving in a circle has acceleration because its direction changes.

Now try this

b Tick (✓) the correct column.

Statement	True	False
i Acceleration is the same as speed.	☐	☐
ii A planet moving round the Sun has acceleration because its direction changes.	☐	☐
iii A car starting from rest and speeding up has acceleration.	☐	☐

Homework

4 In your own words, define acceleration and deceleration.

5 Make a list of **five** objects that show acceleration.

6 Do a calculation to estimate your average acceleration when running from rest.

MOTION REPRESENTED BY GRAPHS

- The **gradient** or slope of a **distance-time graph** is equal to the **speed** of the object.

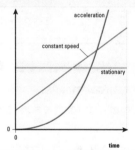

- The gradient or slope of a **velocity-time graph** is equal to **acceleration**.

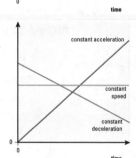

- The area under a velocity-time graph is equal to the **distance** travelled by an object.

Now try this

c Find the following key words in this wordsearch.

speed   time   velocity
gradient   distance

T	A	Y	D	E	E	P	S
T	N	E	I	D	A	R	G
G	T	P	A	P	A	P	T
G	I	G	A	B	I	W	E
D	M	S	I	T	Y	A	E
V	E	L	O	C	I	T	Y
D	I	S	T	A	N	C	E
M	A	M	A	G	T	G	N

TOP TIP Remember gradient = $\dfrac{\text{vertical change}}{\text{horizontal change}}$

Homework

6 Write a short paragraph on distance–time graphs.

7 Write a short paragraph on velocity–time graphs.

8 An object starts from rest and has an acceleration of $5 \ m/s^2$. Determine the speed of the object after 1, 2, 3 seconds and so on up to 10 seconds. Use your results to plot a graph of speed against time. What is the gradient of the graph?

Speed up or slow down

FORCE AND ACCELERATION

- The total **force** acting on an object is known as the **resultant force**.
- An object remains at rest or travels at constant velocity in the same direction when acted upon by a resultant force of zero.
- When a car travels at a steady speed, the **frictional force** balances the **driving force**.
- For an object of a given mass, doubling the resultant force will double the acceleration.
- For a given resultant force, doubling the mass of an object will halve its acceleration.
- resultant force (N) = mass (kg) × acceleration (m/s^2) ($F = ma$)
- Force is measured in newtons (N).
- When two bodies interact, each exerts an equal but opposite force on each other: 'action' = 'reaction'
- The weight of an object is the force of **gravity** acting on the object.
- weight (N) = mass (kg) × gravitational field strength (N/kg)

Now try this

a Tick (✓) the correct column.

Statement	True	False
i Force is measured in kilograms.	☐	☐
ii A hammer hits a nail with a force of 200 N. The nail exerts a force of 200 N in the opposite direction on the hammer.	☐	☐
iii The resultant force on an object travelling at constant velocity is zero.	☐	☐
iv acceleration = $\dfrac{\text{resultant force}}{\text{mass}}$	☐	☐

Homework

1 Using diagrams, illustrate what 'resultant force' means.
2 A car is moving on a level road. Describe all the forces acting on the car.

FALLING

- A falling object in a fluid (liquid or gas) has two forces acting on it: its **weight** (downwards) and **frictional force** (upwards).
- The frictional force due to air is known as **air resistance** or **drag**.
- When an object is dropped, the only force acting on the object is its weight and hence it accelerates at 9.8 m/s^2.
- As the speed of the falling object increases, the frictional force due to the fluid also increases. This decreases the acceleration of the object.
- After some time, the frictional force is equal to the weight of the object. The **resultant force** is zero. The acceleration is also zero and the object has a constant velocity, known as **terminal velocity**.
- acceleration of a falling object =

$$\frac{(\text{weight} - \text{frictional force})}{\text{mass}}$$

Now try this

b Tick (✓) the correct column.

Statement	True	False
i When an object is dropped, the only force acting on it is its weight.	☐	☐
ii An object falling through air has an upward force called drag.	☐	☐
iii Drag decreases as the velocity of the object increases.	☐	☐
iv A stone of weight 1.2 N reaches terminal velocity. The drag is 1.2 N.	☐	☐

 TOP TIP An object falling in air will accelerate as long as the weight and drag are unbalanced.

Homework

3 A skydiver jumps off a helicopter. In your own words, describe how the size of the forces acting on a skydiver change with time.

4 Use the Internet to find the typical terminal speed of a skydiver.

5 Describe why small insects reach terminal velocity very quickly when they fall.

STOP!

- The **thinking distance** is the distance travelled by a car before you actually apply the brakes. (It is the distance travelled in a time equal to the **reaction time** of the driver.)
- The thinking distance is increased if the driver is tired or under the influence of drugs or alcohol, or the car is travelling at a greater speed.
- thinking distance = speed of car × reaction time of driver
- The **braking distance** is the distance travelled by a car as the brakes are applied and the car comes to a halt.
- The braking distance is increased when the road is wet or icy, the brakes are worn, the tyres are bald or the speed of the car is greater.
- **stopping distance** = thinking distance + braking distance

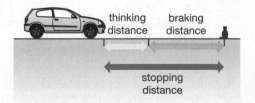

Now try this

c Fill in the missing words.

The reaction time of a driver is 0.6 seconds. The thinking distance when the car is travelling at a speed of 10 m/s is _____ m. Wet conditions will increase the _____ distance and tiredness increases the _____ distance. Driving in wet conditions and being tired will increase the overall _____ distance of the car.

Homework

6 Draw a mind map to show the factors affecting thinking distance.

7 Draw a mind map to show the factors affecting braking distance.

8 Explain why bald tyres increase the braking distance when the road is wet.

Energy, work and momentum

WORK DONE

- A **force** can cause an object to move through a distance. When this happens, **energy** is transferred to the object and **work** is done on the object.
- Work done is measured in **joules** (J).
- Work is the amount of energy transferred when a force moves an object through a certain distance. (Remember: work done on an object = change in energy of object.)
- work done (J) = force (N) × distance moved in the direction of the force (m)

Now try this

a Match the beginning and ending to make complete sentences.

Beginning	Ending
i No work is done on an object if it	joules (J).
ii Work done on an object is always transferred into	newtons (N).
iii Work is measured in	remains stationary.
iv Force is measured in	energy.

 TOP TIP Energy and work are both measured in joules (J).

Homework

1. In your own words, describe work done and how it is related to energy.
2. Draw a mind map for work done.
3. Make a list of situations where a force does work.

ENERGY

- **Conservation of energy**: energy cannot be destroyed or created but it can be changed from one form into another.
- Heat is a form of energy.
- **Work done** against **frictional forces** is usually converted into heat.
- The energy stored in an elastic band or a spring that is stretched is known as **elastic potential energy**.
- Elastic potential energy is stored energy in an object when work is done on the object to change its shape.
- work done (J) against gravity = weight of object (N) × vertical height (m)
- A moving object has **kinetic energy**.
- Kinetic energy is measured in joules (J).
- kinetic energy = $\frac{1}{2}$ × mass × speed² ($KE = \frac{1}{2}mv^2$)

Now try this

b Match each statement with the correct form of energy.

i What type of energy does a person running have?	heat energy
ii What is the energy stored in an extended bungee rope?	kinetic energy
iii What is the energy of the hot brake pads of a car called?	elastic strain energy

Homework

4. Name the different types of energy an object can have. Give an example in each case.
5. Make a list of all the quantities on this page and their associated units.
6. According to a student, the 'kinetic energy of a car is proportional to its speed'. Discuss whether this statement is true or false.

MOMENTUM

- **Momentum** of an object is defined as:
  momentum (kg m/s) = mass (kg) × velocity (m/s)
- Momentum is a **vector quantity**. It has both **magnitude** and **direction**.
- Momentum can have either positive or negative values.

- A **resultant force** acting on an object (for example, a car) will change its momentum.
- In any collision or explosion, providing there are no external forces, momentum is conserved.
- Principle of conservation of momentum:

  total initial momentum of a system = total final momentum of the system
  (This is true as long as there are no external forces acting.)

- Newton's second law:

  $$\text{resultant force} = \frac{\text{change in momentum}}{\text{time taken}}$$

Now try this

c Which of the following statements is/are true?

i Momentum only has direction. _____

ii Momentum depends on both mass and velocity. _____

iii In a collision, both momentum and total energy are conserved. _____

iv Momentum increases with the mass of an object. _____

Homework

7 Give **four** examples of an object having momentum.

8 Give **four** examples of collisions and describe what quantity is conserved.

9 Discuss the quantities conserved in all collisions.

CARS AND MOMENTUM

- The safety features in cars are **seatbelts**, **airbags** and **crumple zones**. They change shape, reduce injuries and absorb energy.
- Seatbelts prevent collisions with the dashboard and windscreen.
- Seatbelts, airbags and crumple zones increase a person's time for stopping. For a given change in momentum, this means a smaller force is acting on the person.
- Airbags inflate rapidly during a collision. They prevent collisions with the dashboard and steering wheel.

Now try this

d Circle all the safety features of a car.

steering wheel

tyres

seatbelts

wipers

airbags

crumple zone

Homework

10 Make a list of the safety features in a car and describe how they reduce injuries.

11 Have a look at your parents' or a friend's car. Make a list of its safety features.

12 Explain why airbags have holes to let air out during an impact.

Static electricity

CHARGING INSULATORS

- Rubbing can **charge insulators** such as wool, plastic and rubber.
- When two insulators rub against each other, the **friction** between them causes some of the outer **electrons** of the atoms to be stripped off one of the insulators.
- An insulator acquires a charge by transfer of electrons.
- An insulator becomes negative when it gains electrons.
- An insulator that loses electrons will have a positive charge.
- Like (similar) charges **repel**. Unlike (opposite) charges attract.
- A polythene rod rubbed with a duster acquires a negative charge and the duster acquires an equal but opposite negative charge.

 TOP TIP Electrical charges can move easily through metals.

Now try this

a Tick (✓) the correct answer.

  i An insulator becomes positive because it gains protons. ☐

  ii All insulators can be charged by friction. ☐

  iii Two positively charged balloons attract each other. ☐

  iv Two negative electrons will repel each other. ☐

Homework

1. Explain how insulators can acquire a positive or negative charge.
2. Make a list of objects or items in your house where dust sticks to surfaces because of electrostatic attraction.
3. Describe what happens when you bring a charged comb or cling film near to a dripping tap.

ELECTRIC SPARKS

- As the **charge** on an isolated **insulator** increases, so does the **potential difference** between the insulator and the Earth.
- When the potential difference between the charged object and the Earth becomes too large, electrons and other charges can be transferred through the air as an **electric spark**.

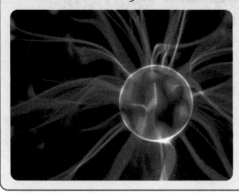

- Electric sparks can generate high temperatures and are therefore dangerous near petrol fumes (for example, refuelling aircraft).
- Earthing an object can reduce electric sparks.

Now try this

b Complete the sentences by filling in the missing words.

An electric _____ is created when charges are transferred between an object and the ground through the _____. Electric sparks are very _____ because they increase the temperature of the air. Electric sparks can easily ignite petrol _____.

Homework

4. Make a list of places where electric sparks can be extremely dangerous.
5. In your own words, describe how an electric spark is produced.
6. Make a list of items where sparks are useful.

THE USES OF ELECTROSTATICS

- An **electrostatic precipitator** removes dangerous smoke from chimneys.
- In coal-burning power stations, smoke particles (soot) in the chimney are removed by first charging them and then attracting them to oppositely-charged metal plates.
- **Electrostatics** is used in paint spraying.
- Electrostatic attraction is used in photocopiers.
- This is how a photocopier works:
  - the image is projected onto a light-sensitive (selenium) drum
  - only the dark sections of the drum become positively charged
  - fine black powder (toner) is negatively charged and this sticks to the positive sections of the drum
  - the black powdered image is transferred to paper by contact
  - the image is 'fixed' on the paper by heating it.

Now try this

c Find the following key words linked to photocopiers in this wordsearch.

light   heating   image
powder   drum

W	E	R	K	A	V	A	L
T	H	G	I	L	Z	D	L
X	E	L	T	V	D	P	A
N	A	D	R	U	M	O	S
E	T	H	W	G	F	W	E
E	I	F	X	P	U	D	R
T	N	I	M	A	G	E	B
U	G	C	S	A	S	R	J

 Remember that opposite charges attract.

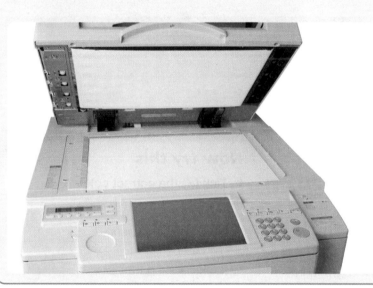

Homework

7 Draw a labelled diagram of a smoke precipitator.

8 Draw a block diagram to show how an image is produced on a sheet of paper in a photocopier.

9 Describe how spray painting gives an even coat and uses less paint.

Currents in circuits

CIRCUITS

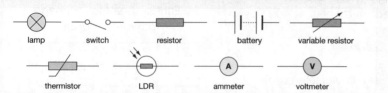

- A complete loop is required for an **electrical circuit** to work.
- The size of the **current** for a given circuit depends on the **resistance**.
- A **variable resistor** can be used to change the resistance in a circuit and hence the current.

 TOP TIP A circuit will not work if there is a break in the circuit.

Now try this

a Complete the following sentences.

A battery is connected to a lamp. The lamp is brightly lit because the circuit is c_____. The lamp is replaced by another lamp of greater resistance. The current in the circuit now is I_____ and the lamp will be d_____.

Homework

1 Design **two** simple circuits with lamps. Explain what each circuit does.
2 Design a circuit for switching on two lamps independently.
3 Design a circuit to change the brightness of a lamp.

RESISTANCE

- **Electric current** is the rate of flow of **charge**.
- In a **circuit**, electric current is due to the movement of **electrons**.
- Current is measured using an **ammeter** placed in series with a component. It is measured in **amperes** (A).
- **Potential difference** (pd) is measured using a **voltmeter** placed in parallel with a component. It is measured in **volts** (V).
- The **resistance** of a component is found using the equation:

$$\text{resistance } (\Omega) = \frac{\text{potential difference (V)}}{\text{current (A)}} \qquad R = \frac{V}{I}$$

- Resistance is measured in **ohms** (Ω).
- potential difference (V) = current (A) × resistance (Ω) or $V = IR$

Now try this

b Tick (✓) the correct column.

Statement	True	False
i Current is measured in amperes.	☐	☐
ii Decreasing the resistance will decrease the current in a circuit.	☐	☐
iii A 12 V lamp carrying a current of 6.0 A has a resistance of 2.0 Ω.	☐	☐
iv Potential difference is the same as current.	☐	☐

Homework

4 Write a few sentences on current, potential difference and resistance.
5 Make a list of electrical quantities and their associated units.
6 Draw a table of an electrical device (for example, a computer monitor) in your home and its operating pd and current. Calculate the resistance of the device.

COMPONENTS

- A given **resistor** will have a constant **resistance**.
- The **current** in a resistor at a constant temperature is directly proportional to the **potential difference** across the resistor.
- The resistance of a filament lamp increases with the temperature of the filament.
- The current in a **diode** is in one direction only.
- A diode has infinite resistance in the 'reverse' direction.
- The following current-potential difference graphs are important:

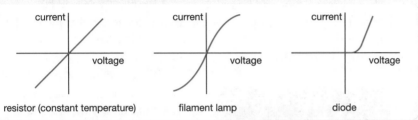

resistor (constant temperature)   filament lamp   diode

- The resistance of a **NTC (negative temperature coefficient) thermistor** decreases as its temperature increases.
- The resistance of a **light-dependent resistor (LDR)** decreases as the intensity of light increases.

Now try this

c Circle the components below that change their resistance when the temperature is changed.

filament lamp

resistor

ammeter

voltmeter

switch

thermistor

Homework

7   In your own words, describe how current affects the resistance of a resistor.

8   In your own words, explain how current affects the resistance of a filament lamp.

9   Write a short paragraph on diodes.

SERIES AND PARALLEL

- For a **series circuit**:
  - the total resistance is the sum of the resistances of the components.
  - the current in each component is the same.
  - the total potential difference across the components is equal to the sum of the potential differences across each component.
- For a **parallel circuit**:
  - the potential difference across each component is the same.
  - the total current in a circuit is equal to the sum of the currents in each component.

Now try this

d The following components are connected to a given battery. Use up ↑ and down ↓ arrows to indicate what happens to the current in the circuit.

i   A high resistance resistor is swapped with a resistor of low resistance.

ii The temperature of a thermistor is decreased.

iii The temperature of a thermistor is increased.

iv An extra lamp is connected in the circuit.

Homework

10   Draw a mind map for a series circuit.

11   Draw a mind map for a parallel circuit.

12   You are given resistors of values 10Ω, 20Ω, and 30Ω. Show how you can get different total resistance values.

Mains electricity and power

DOMESTIC ELECTRICITY

- A **cell** or a **battery** produces a **direct current** (DC).
- The direction of direct current does not change.
- An **alternating current** (AC) continuously changes direction.
- The **domestic mains electricity** is an alternating current supply.
- In the UK, the domestic mains supply is about 230 V and has a frequency of 50 cycles per second, or 50 Hz.
- The high potential difference (230 V) provided by the mains electricity can lead to serious shocks, severe burns and can also be fatal.
- An **oscilloscope** can be used to show an alternating potential difference across a component.

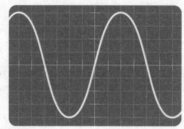

- The frequency of an alternating potential difference is related to the period by the equation:

$$\text{frequency (Hz)} = \frac{1}{\text{period (s)}}$$

Now try this

a Place a tick (✓) at the end of each statement if it is correct.

  i The mains electricity has a frequency of 230 Hz. ☐

  ii A cell used in a torch provides direct current. ☐

  iii An alternating current changes direction. ☐

  iv The mains electricity can be extremely dangerous. ☐

TOP TIP The time taken for one complete cycle is called the period.

Homework

1 Make a list of all the appliances in your home that use mains electricity.

2 Using diagrams, explain to a friend what is meant by a direct current and an alternating current.

3 A table lamp is connected to the mains supply that alternates at a rate of 50 Hz. Explain why the lamp does not flicker.

SAFETY AT HOME

- An **electrical cable** has three coloured wires: brown, blue and green/yellow.
- All domestic appliances have a **three-pin plug**.
- The brown wire leads to the **live terminal**, the blue wire to the **neutral terminal** and the green/yellow wire to the **earth terminal**.
- The live wire of the mains supply alternates between negative and positive potentials with respect to the neutral terminal.
- The neutral terminal of the mains supply stays close to zero volts.
- Metal appliances are **earthed** in order to protect you from accidental shocks.
- An earthed conductor cannot become live.
- **Double-insulated appliances** have plastic casing and do not need to be earthed.
- The **fuse** is attached to the live terminal.
- The fuse is a safety device. A large current will melt the fuse and cut off the supply.
- A fuse prevents large currents from starting a fire.
- **Circuit breakers** are safety devices and can be described as 'resettable fuses'.

Now try this

b The diagram shows a mains three-pin plug. What is wrong with the plug?

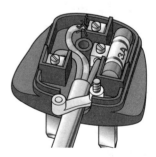

TOP TIP A fuse has to be replaced after a fault, but circuit breakers just have to be reset.

Homework

4 In your own words, describe how a fuse prevents electrical fires.

5 Write a short paragraph to explain the purpose of earthing an appliance.

6 Make a list of double-insulated items in your home or in a friend's home.

WHICH FUSE?

- An **electric current** is due to the flow of **charge**.
- Electric charge is measured in **coulombs** (C).
- When charge flows through a **resistor**, electrical energy is transformed into heat.
- **Power** is the rate at which energy is transformed. That is:

$$\text{power (W)} = \frac{\text{energy transferred (J)}}{\text{time (s)}}$$

- **Electrical power**, **potential difference** and current are related by the equation:

$$\text{power (W) = current (A)} \times \text{potential difference (V)}$$
$$P = VI$$

- The equation:

$$I = \frac{P}{V}$$

can be used to find the **fuse** rating for a particular domestic appliance.
- The energy transformed into heat is related to the potential difference and the amount of charge by the equation:

$$\text{energy transformed (J) = potential difference (V)} \times \text{charge (C)}$$

- The amount of charge flow at a point in a circuit is related to the current and the time by the equation:

$$\text{charge (C) = current (A)} \times \text{time (s)}$$

Now try this

c Match the quantity on the left-hand side with the correct unit on the right-hand side.

i charge   watt

ii current   joule

iii potential difference   coulomb

iv energy   volt

v power   ampere

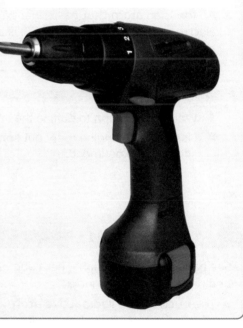

Homework

7 Draw a table of all the electrical appliances in your home and their power ratings.

Use $I = \dfrac{P}{V}$ to determine the correct fuse rating for each appliance.

8 Make revision cards of all the equations in this section.

9 Make a list of all the quantities and their associated units.

Nuclear physics

INSIDE THE ATOM

- The **alpha scattering experiment** of Rutherford and Marsden:
  - showed that an **atom** has a very small, massive and positive nucleus
  - the alpha particles were directed towards a thin gold foil
  - some of the alpha particles were scattered through unexpected large angles – the 'plum-pudding' model of the atom could not have explained this, the large scatter of the alpha particles could only be explained by the positive alpha particles being repelled by a tiny but massive, positive nucleus of the gold atom
  - most of the alpha particles showed no scattering, which confirmed that most of the space of the atom was a vacuum
- The **nucleus** of an atom contains **protons** and **neutrons** and is surrounded by electrons.
- In a neutral atom, the number of protons is equal to the number of electrons.
- An **ion** is an atom that has either gained electrons or lost electrons. An ion is a **charged** atom.

Now try this

a Circle all the particles that have a charge.

electron

atom

ion

proton

neutron

alpha particle

Particle	Mass relative to a proton	Charge relative to a proton
proton	1	+1
neutron	1	0
electron	$1/1830 \approx 0$	−1

Homework

1. Write a paragraph to outline the important conclusions of the alpha scattering experiment.
2. Use a search engine to try out some animations called applets by typing in 'applets alpha scattering experiment'.

RADIOACTIVITY

See page 36, Panel 1 (Alpha, beta and gamma) for a definition of an isotope and representation of nuclei.

- The **nucleus** of a **radioactive atom** emits either an **alpha (α) particle** or a **beta (β) particle** and/or **gamma (γ) rays**.
- An alpha particle is a **helium nucleus** ($^4_2$He) and has a **positive charge**. It has two neutrons and two protons.
- A beta particle is an **electron** and has a **negative charge**.
- Gamma rays are short-wavelength **electromagnetic waves** and have no charge.
- In alpha **decay**, the **mass number** decreases by four and the **proton number** decreases by two, forming a new **radioisotope**.
- In beta decay, the mass number remains the same and the proton number increases by one, forming a new radioisotope.
- There is no change to the mass or proton number after emission of gamma rays from the nucleus.
- **Background radiation** is always present and is due to radioactive substances in rocks, soil and air, and **cosmic rays**.

Now try this

b Complete the sentences by filling in the missing words.

An isotope of uranium has 143 neutrons and 92 protons. Its mass number is _____. The nucleus decays by emitting an alpha particle. The nucleus left behind has a proton number of _____ and a mass number of _____.

Homework

3 Use the Internet to find the isotopes of **three** elements.

4 Write a few sentences on the nucleus, isotopes and alpha particles.

5 Suggest why radioactivity cannot be destroyed by chemical reactions.

FISSION AND FUSION

- **Nuclear reactors** use **uranium-235** and/or **plutonium-239** as fuel.
- **Nuclear fission** is the splitting of an atomic nucleus.
- Fission in uranium-235 or plutonium-239 nuclei occurs when a **neutron** is absorbed.
- In a fission reaction, a neutron is captured by a uranium-235 nucleus and it splits into two smaller (daughter) nuclei and either two or three neutrons.
- Energy is released when a uranium nucleus splits.
- In a **chain reaction**, the neutrons can cause further fission reactions.
- In **nuclear fusion**, two atomic nuclei join together to form a larger nucleus.
- Energy is released in a fusion reaction.
- Stars produce their energy from nuclear fusion reactions.

Now try this

c For each statement, tick (✓) the correct column.

Statement	True	False
i Fission reactions release chemical energy.	☐	☐
ii Fission means splitting of a nucleus.	☐	☐
iii Fission is used in atomic bombs and nuclear power stations.	☐	☐
iv Fusion takes place in stars.	☐	☐

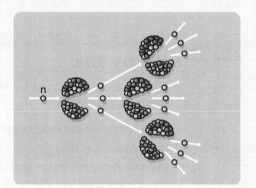

Homework

6 With the help of a labelled diagram, describe a chain reaction.

7 Write a short paragraph to describe the differences and the similarities between fusion reactions and fission reactions.

8 Write a short paragraph to describe the similarities between fusion and fission reactions.

Exchange

ACTIVE TRANSPORT

- Cells must sometimes take in substances against a **concentration gradient**.
- Substances move in the opposite direction to normal **diffusion**.
- Substances move from an area of low concentration to an area of higher concentration.
- This process of **active transport** requires energy from respiration.
- Root hair cells absorb mineral ions from a very dilute solution in the soil by active transport.
- In humans, sugar from a low concentration in the kidney tubules may be absorbed back into the blood by active transport.

Now Try This

a Answer the following by writing diffusion (D), osmosis (O) or active transport (A).

_____ Involves the movement of water molecules.

_____ Occurs along a concentration gradient.

_____ Occurs against a concentration gradient.

_____ Is passive.

_____ Requires energy from respiration.

_____ Accumulates substances within cells.

 TOP TIP Active transport is like pushing a ball up a hill, it requires energy.

Homework

1 List the main differences between active transport and diffusion.
2 Why is active transport necessary in root hair cells?
3 Why is active transport necessary in the kidney tubule?

SURFACE AREA

- Many organs in plants and animals are **specialised** for exchanging materials.
- **Exchange** occurs at a surface, for example the cell membrane.
- The surface controls what can pass through and how quickly.
- The more **surface area** available at an exchange surface, the quicker the rate of exchange.
- In the small intestine, the exchange surface is highly folded into **villi**.

- The villi increase the surface area.
- This allows quicker **absorption** of food molecules by diffusion and active transport.

 TOP TIP Many small folds or pockets give a large surface area.

Now Try This

b Complete the passage by filling in the missing words.

Many plant and animal organs are specialised for the _____ of substances. Exchange surfaces often have a large _____ _____. This allows _____ and _____ _____ to occur more quickly. For example, the surface of the small _____ is highly folded into many _____. This gives a _____ surface area for the _____ of food molecules.

Homework

4 Explain how the small intestine is specialised for absorbing food molecules.
5 Describe an example of an exchange surface with a large surface area in plants.
6 Explain how a large surface area helps with the exchange of substances.

LEAVES AND ROOTS

- **Carbon dioxide** enters plants via **diffusion** into the leaves.
- **Stomata** (pores) on the underside of leaves allow carbon dioxide to enter.
- Leaves have a flattened shape, which gives a large surface area for the diffusion of carbon dioxide and to capture sunlight.
- Internal **air spaces** allow carbon dioxide to diffuse within the leaf to photosynthesising cells.
- Water and mineral ions enter leaves via the roots.
- Roots have a large surface area due to their long, thin shape.
- **Root hairs** further increase the surface area for absorption of water and minerals.

 Plants absorb water from the soil by osmosis.

Now Try This

c Circle the correct answer.

Water enters the plant through the:
leaves   stem   roots

Stomata are found on the:
leaves   stem   roots

Mineral ions enter the plant through the:
leaves   stem   roots

Carbon dioxide enters the plant by:
diffusion   osmosis   active transport

Mineral ions enter the plant by:
diffusion   osmosis   active transport

Water enters the plant by:
diffusion   osmosis   active transport

Homework

7 Describe how a leaf is specialised for photosynthesis.

8 Describe how the roots are specialised for absorption of water and minerals.

9 How do plants use diffusion and osmosis to exchange materials with their surroundings?

TRANSPIRATION

- **Transpiration** is when **water vapour** evaporates from the surface of leaves.
- Most transpiration occurs through the **stomata** on the underside of leaves.
- Each stoma is surrounded by a pair of **guard cells**.
- Guard cells open and close the stomata depending on conditions such as light, water availability and temperature.
- Stomata are usually open during the day and closed at night.
- Most water is lost in very hot, dry and windy conditions.
- In hot, dry weather the stomata may close to prevent too much water loss.

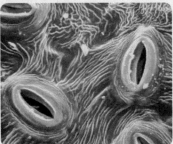

Now Try This

d Match the statements on the right-hand side with the three parts of a plant.

stomata   i   Anchor the plant in the ground.

    ii   Allow oxygen to diffuse out of the plant.

    iii   Absorb sunlight energy for photosynthesis.

leaves   iv   Absorb mineral ions by active transport.

    v   Allow carbon dioxide to enter the plant.

    vi   Make glucose by photosynthesis.

roots   vii   Absorb water by osmosis.

    viii   Surrounded by a pair of guard cells.

Homework

10 Why are stomata found on the underside of leaves?

11 Why are stomata usually open during the day and closed at night?

12 Draw a labelled diagram to show a stoma and two guard cells.

Breathing

THE BREATHING SYSTEM

- The **breathing system** is also known as the **respiratory system**.
- The organs of the breathing system are found in the **thorax** (chest cavity).
- The thorax is separated from the abdomen by the **diaphragm**.
- Air from the mouth passes down the **trachea**.
- The trachea splits into two **bronchi**, each supplying a **lung**.
- Each bronchus splits into many tiny tubes called **bronchioles**.
- Each bronchiole ends in a tiny sac called an **alveolus**.
- The ribcage protects the heart and the breathing system.

 Do not confuse the trachea (windpipe) and the oesophagus (food pipe) – they are completely different tubes!

Now Try This

a Match each part of the breathing system to its description.

i Tiny sacs where gas exchange takes place.   ribcage

ii Protects the heart and lungs.   rib muscles

iii Sheet of muscle that flattens as it contracts.   alveoli

iv Raise and lower the ribcage.   bronchus

v Carries air from the trachea to each lung.   bronchioles

vi Tiny tubes that carry air to the alveoli.   diaphragm

Homework

1 Draw a flowchart to show the pathway of air from the mouth to the alveoli.

2 Explain the purpose of breathing.

3 Sketch a labelled diagram showing the main parts of the breathing system.

VENTILATION

- Air is taken into and out of the body by the breathing system.
- When we **inhale**:
  - the **rib muscles** move the **ribcage** outwards and upwards.
  - the **diaphragm** muscle flattens, increasing the volume inside the **thorax**.
  - the pressure outside is greater than the pressure inside the thorax.
  - air is drawn into the lungs.
- When we **exhale**:
  - the ribcage moves downwards and inwards.
  - the diaphragm returns to its domed shape.
  - the volume inside the thorax decreases.
  - the pressure inside the thorax increases and forces air out of the lungs.

Now Try This

b Cross out the incorrect answer to leave the correct answer.

When we breathe in...

the rib muscles **contract/relax**.

the ribcage is **lowered/raised**.

the volume inside the chest **increases/decreases**.

the pressure outside is **greater/less** than the pressure inside.

the diaphragm is **domed/flattened**.

air rushes **in/out** of the lungs.

Homework

4 Why may a broken rib make breathing difficult?

5 Write a paragraph to explain what happens when we inhale.

6 Write a paragraph to explain what happens when we exhale.

ALVEOLI

- The air we inhale contains the **oxygen** required for **respiration**.
- At the **alveoli**, oxygen diffuses into the bloodstream and carbon dioxide diffuses out.
- This process is called **gas exchange**.
- A network of tiny blood **capillaries** surrounds each alveolus.
- Oxygen diffuses from the alveoli into the **red blood cells**.
- The bloodstream carries this oxygen to respiring cells all around the body.
- **Carbon dioxide** is a waste product of respiration.

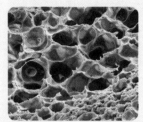

- Carbon dioxide is carried in the blood **plasma** from respiring cells to the lungs.
- At the alveoli, carbon dioxide diffuses from the blood into the lungs where it is exhaled.

 Alveoli is the plural form. In the singular it is one alveolus.

Now Try This

c Air we breathe in contains _____ which our cells need for respiration. Oxygen in the alveolus _____ through the walls of the alveolus and _____ into the _____. The blood is now said to be _____. At the same time,

_____ _____

diffuses in the opposite direction, and is removed from the lungs as we _____.

Homework

7 Describe the pathway of oxygen from the air to a respiring cell.

8 Describe the pathway of carbon dioxide from a respiring cell to the lungs.

9 Explain the role of diffusion in gas exchange.

THE LUNGS AS AN EXCHANGE SURFACE

- The **alveoli** provide a **very large surface area** for **diffusion**.
- The alveoli are surrounded by a dense network of tiny blood **capillaries**.
- This brings the bloodstream into close contact with the air in the alveoli so that oxygen and carbon dioxide have only a short distance to diffuse.
- The walls of the alveoli and blood capillaries are very thin, making it easier for the oxygen and carbon dioxide to diffuse across.
- There is a thin film of moisture on the inside of each alveolus.
- Oxygen dissolves in this moisture before it diffuses through.
- The moisture also prevents the lungs from drying out.

 Blood capillary walls are only one cell thick.

Now Try This

d Find the following keywords in this wordsearch.

alveolus   oxygen   diffusion   lung
inhale   bronchi   ribcage   trachea

R	I	A	O	O	R	D	E	J
I	N	U	X	Z	X	I	W	T
B	H	X	Y	B	P	F	A	R
C	A	I	G	R	O	F	X	A
A	L	V	E	O	L	U	S	C
G	E	T	N	N	U	S	S	H
E	V	B	L	C	N	I	V	E
M	V	C	N	H	G	O	D	A
G	B	Y	H	I	Q	N	F	K

Homework

10 Research and write a paragraph on the effect of emphysema on the alveoli.

11 Describe **two** features of the alveoli that help gas exchange.

12 Explain the purpose of having a large surface area in the lungs.

Circulation

THE DOUBLE CIRCULATION

- Substances are transported around the body by the **circulatory system**.
- The circulatory system consists of the **heart** which acts as a pump, **blood vessels** and **blood**.
- In humans, there is a **double circulation system**.
- For each circulation around the body, the blood passes through the heart twice.
- One circuit pumps blood to the lungs to pick up oxygen.
- The other pumps blood to the rest of the body to supply cells with glucose and oxygen.

 TOP TIP The right side of the heart pumps blood to the lungs, the left pumps blood to the body.

Now Try This

a Put these sentences in the correct order.

☐	Blood picks up oxygen from the lungs.
☐	The heart pumps oxygenated blood to the rest of the body.
☐	The heart pumps deoxygenated blood to the lungs.
☐	Oxygenated blood travels back to the heart.
1	Veins carry deoxygenated blood back to the heart.
☐	The blood is said to be oxygenated.

Homework

1 Describe the pathway of a red blood cell around the body.

2 Why is a double circulatory system necessary in large mammals such as humans?

3 Research and write a paragraph on **one** example of a single circulatory system.

THE HEART

- The **heart** is made of **cardiac muscle**, which never gets tired.
- The heart is made of four **chambers**:

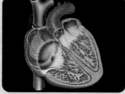

  - the two upper chambers are called the **atria**, this is where blood enters the heart.
  - the two lower chambers are called the **ventricles**, the wall of the left ventricle is thicker than that of the right.
- **Valves** ensure blood flows in the correct direction around the heart.
- The right side of the heart receives **deoxygenated blood** from the body and pumps it to the **lungs**.
- The left side receives **oxygenated blood** from the lungs and pumps it around the body.
- The two sides of the heart are completely separate so that oxygenated and deoxygenated blood never mix.

Now Try This

b Match each question to its correct answer.

i	Upper chamber of the heart.	valves
ii	Organ that pumps blood around the body.	left
iii	This side of the heart is the biggest.	heart
iv	Colour which represents oxygenated blood.	red
v	Colour which represents deoxygenated blood.	atrium
vi	These stop blood from flowing the wrong way in the heart.	blue

Homework

4 Why is the wall of the left ventricle thicker than that of the right?

5 Why is it important that the right and left sides of the heart are kept separate?

6 Research and write a paragraph on holes in the heart.

See pages 20–23 of Collins GCSE Biology

BLOOD VESSELS

- There are three types of **blood vessel**: **arteries**, **veins** and **capillaries**.
- Arteries carry **oxygenated blood** from the heart to the rest of the body.
- Arteries have thick elastic walls to withstand the high pressure of the blood flowing through them.
- Veins carry **deoxygenated blood** from the organs of the body back to the heart.
- Blood in veins is under low pressure so they have **valves** to ensure that blood flows in the correct direction.
- Tiny blood vessels called **capillaries** supply blood to the organs.
- Capillaries are only one cell thick so that substances can easily pass from the blood to the organs and vice versa.

 Remember! **A**rteries carry blood **a**way from the heart.

Now Try This

c Write arteries (A), veins (V) or capillaries (C) next to the following statements.

Carry blood to the heart. _____

Carry blood away from the heart. _____

Thick elastic walls. _____

Walls one cell thick. _____

Carry blood under high pressure. _____

Carry blood under low pressure. _____

Thin muscular walls. _____

Have valves. _____

Carry deoxygenated blood. _____

Carry oxygenated blood. _____

Homework

7 Why is blood flowing through arteries under higher pressure than in the veins?

8 Explain the purpose of valves in veins.

9 Will capillaries contain oxygenated or deoxygenated blood? Explain your answer.

BLOOD

- **Blood** is a tissue made up of several different components.
- **Red blood cells** transport **oxygen**.
- They contain the red pigment **haemoglobin**.
- At the lungs, haemoglobin binds reversibly to oxygen to form **oxyhaemoglobin**.
- At respiring cells, the oxyhaemoglobin splits up to release oxygen for respiration.
- The blood **plasma** is a straw coloured liquid.
- It transports **carbon dioxide**, **urea** and the soluble products of digestion.
- The **white blood cells** are involved in fighting infections.
- **Platelets** are cell fragments which are involved in the **clotting** process.

 Red blood cells contain no nucleus to leave more room for carrying oxygen.

Now Try This

d Circle the correct answer.

Red blood cells carry:

   oxygen   carbon dioxide   glucose

White blood cells are involved in:

   transport   fighting disease   clotting

Clotting is carried out by the:

   red cells   white cells   platelets

Red blood cells contain:

   nuclei   haemoglobin   platelets

Blood plasma transports:

   oxygen   haemoglobin   carbon dioxide

Glucose is transported in the:

   red cells   white cells   plasma

Homework

10 Describe how red blood cells are specialised for their function.

11 Explain why the reaction between oxygen and haemoglobin must be reversible.

12 Write a paragraph on the functions of blood plasma.

Exercise and respiration

EXERCISE AND ENERGY

- **Energy** from **respiration** is used in muscle **contraction**, which enables us to move.
- When we exercise, the increase in movement means that more energy is required.
- This extra energy comes from an increased rate of respiration in the muscles.
- Blood flow to the muscles increases in order to supply them with the extra glucose and oxygen required for respiration.
- The heart rate increases in order to pump blood more quickly to the muscles.
- The rate and depth of breathing increase to:
  - increase the amount of oxygen entering the blood.
  - remove the extra carbon dioxide produced.

Now Try This

a Circle the correct answer.

Energy is released for muscle contraction by:
    exercise   breathing   respiration

Respiration requires a supply of:
    oxygen   carbon dioxide   water

Respiration produces the waste product:
    glucose   carbon dioxide   oxygen

The extra oxygen required is obtained by:
    breathing   respiration   exercise

The carbon dioxide produced is removed via:
    urine   sweat   exhaling

Homework

1 List **three** effects of exercise on the body.
2 Explain why the breathing rate increases during exercise.
3 Explain why the heart rate increases during exercise.

ANAEROBIC RESPIRATION

- During vigorous exercise, the heart and lungs cannot get enough oxygen to the muscles quickly enough to supply the increased rate of respiration.
- The muscles still need to release energy but have to do so without oxygen.
- **Anaerobic respiration** is respiration without oxygen:
  glucose → lactic acid + carbon dioxide
- The glucose molecule is only partially broken down to release some of the energy it contains.
- This energy is released in a quick burst.
- **Lactic acid** builds up in the muscles causing cramp and fatigue.
- Lactic acid is **toxic** and must be removed from the muscles.

 TOP TIP Less energy is released in anaerobic respiration than in aerobic respiration.

Now Try This

b Write aerobic (A) or anaerobic (An) to answer the following.

Releases energy steadily. _____

Releases energy in a quick burst. _____

Occurs in the mitochondria. _____

Involves the incomplete breakdown of glucose. _____

Requires oxygen. _____

Releases only a small amount of energy. _____

Produces water as a by-product. _____

Homework

4 Prepare a table comparing aerobic and anaerobic respiration.
5 Explain the effects on the body of anaerobic respiration.
6 Research and write a paragraph about the effects of lactic acid on the body.

THE OXYGEN DEBT

- The **lactic acid** released during **anaerobic respiration** is toxic and must be removed from the muscles.
- The lactic acid is **oxidised** to produce carbon dioxide and water.
- This oxidation releases the energy remaining in the lactic acid molecule.
- The extra oxygen required to oxidise the lactic acid is called the **oxygen debt**.
- Extra oxygen must be transported to the muscles in order to oxidise the lactic acid and repay the oxygen debt.
- After exercise, the **breathing rate** and **heart rate** do not return to normal immediately.
- The increased breathing rate is required to obtain the extra oxygen needed and remove the carbon dioxide produced.

Now Try This

c Complete the passage by filling in the missing words.

During vigorous exercise, the heart and lungs cannot get enough _____ to the muscles. Without oxygen they undergo _____ _____. This involves the _____ breakdown of glucose to release a _____ amount of _____ in a _____ burst. _____ acid is produced. This is called the _____ debt. After exercise, the _____ and _____ rates remain high to intake extra oxygen to _____ the lactic acid to _____ _____ and _____.

Homework

7 Explain why long-distance runners must run at a slower speed than sprinters.

8 Explain what is meant by the term 'oxygen debt'.

9 Explain why the breathing rate remains high for some time after exercise.

YEAST

- Yeast is a single-celled organism with a nucleus, cytoplasm, cell membrane and cell wall.
- Yeast can respire aerobically (with oxygen) or anaerobically (without oxygen).
- In the presence of oxygen, yeast respire aerobically which involves the complete breakdown of glucose molecules.
- Aerobic respiration produces more energy and is needed for normal growth:
  glucose + oxygen → carbon dioxide + water + energy
- Anaerobic respiration involves the incomplete breakdown of glucose molecules and so releases less energy than aerobic respiration.
- Anaerobic respiration in yeast is called **fermentation**:
  glucose → ethanol + carbon dioxide + energy

Now Try This

d How much do you know about yeast? Answer true (T) or false (F) to the following statements.

Yeast cells have a cell wall. _____

Yeast only respire anaerobically. _____

Yeast cells can produce alcohol. _____

Yeast cells produce lactic acid. _____

Yeast require oxygen for normal growth. _____

Respiration in yeast produces carbon dioxide. _____

Yeast build up an oxygen debt. _____

Homework

10 Explain the difference between aerobic and anaerobic respiration.

11 Explain why aerobic respiration releases more energy than anaerobic respiration.

12 Why do you think yeast can respire both aerobically and anaerobically?

The kidneys

CLEANING THE BLOOD

- The **kidneys** are the part of the **excretory system** which removes the waste products of the body's **metabolism**.
- The kidneys filter the blood to remove any waste products which would otherwise build up in the blood and become toxic.
- For example, the kidneys remove **urea** which is produced by the **deamination** of excess **amino acids** in the **liver**.
- Excess water and ions are also removed from the blood.
- The waste filtered out of the blood by the kidneys is known as **urine**.
- Each kidney passes urine down a **ureter** to be stored in the **bladder**.
- Periodically the bladder is emptied and the urine passes down the **urethra** and out of the body.

Now Try This

a Match each word to the correct description.

i	Pair of organs that 'clean' the blood.	urea
ii	Removal of waste products of the body's metabolism.	kidneys
iii	Carries urine from a kidney to the bladder.	ureter
iv	Waste product from the deamination of excess amino acids.	urethra
v	Urine passes through this tube to outside the body.	excretion

Homework

1. List **three** things that are removed from the blood by the kidneys.
2. Sketch a diagram showing the kidneys, ureters, bladder and urethra.
3. Explain the purpose of the bladder.

STAGES OF FILTRATION

- Blood arrives at the **glomerulus** under high pressure.
- Small molecules, such as urea and glucose, are squeezed through the wall of the **capillary** and **Bowman's capsule** and into the **nephron**. This is called **ultrafiltration**.
- Cells and large molecules, such as proteins, are too big and remain in the blood.
- At the loop, **selective reabsorption** occurs.
- Useful substances, such as glucose, some water and some ions, are reabsorbed into the blood.
- Some substances must be **actively reabsorbed** against a **concentration gradient**, for example glucose.
- At the **collecting duct**, the remaining liquid drains through to the **ureter**.
- This is the **urine**, which contains excess water, excess ions and all urea.

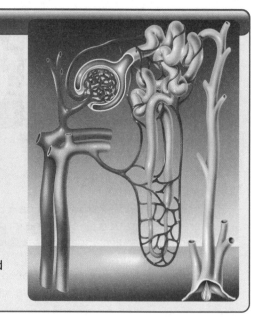

Homework

4. List **three** substances that may be selectively reabsorbed by the kidneys.
5. Explain the role of active transport in kidney function.
6. Why is urea not selectively reabsorbed?

TOP TIP Molecules move through the walls of the capillary and Bowman's capsule by diffusion.

ADH AND WATER REGULATION

- The reabsorption of water by the kidneys is controlled by the hormone **ADH**.
- ADH is secreted by the **pituitary gland**.
- When the blood contains too little water:
  - the pituitary gland detects the concentration of the blood.
  - ADH is secreted into the bloodstream.
  - ADH causes more water to be reabsorbed at the **kidney tubules**.
  - a small volume of concentrated urine is produced.
- When the blood contains too much water:
  - the pituitary gland suppresses secretion of ADH.
  - less water is reabsorbed at the kidney tubules.
  - a large volume of dilute urine is produced.

 TOP TIP ADH = antidiuretic hormone

Now Try This

b Cross out the incorrect answer leaving the correct answer.

When the blood water level is too high:

The pituitary gland **suppresses/secretes** ADH.

More/less ADH is released into the bloodstream.

More/less water is reabsorbed into the blood.

A **large/small** amount of urine is produced.

The urine is **concentrated/dilute.**

Homework

7 Describe what happens when the water content of the blood becomes too high.

8 Describe what happens when the water content of the blood becomes too low.

9 Explain what a hormone is.

KIDNEY FAILURE

- If both **kidneys** fail, a patient will die without either **dialysis** or a **transplant**.
- In dialysis, blood from a patient's vein is passed through a dialysis machine.
- A dialysis machine contains a **partially permeable membrane** separating the blood from **dialysis fluid**.
- The dialysis fluid contains the ideal amount of water and ions that the blood should contain.
- Waste diffuses from the patient's blood into the dialysis fluid.
- Kidney transplants replace a lost or diseased kidney with a healthy one.

- **Donor kidneys** can be rejected by the body's **immune system**.
- A donated kidney should have a similar tissue type to the patient to reduce the risk of rejection.
- Treatment with drugs to suppress the immune system may help prevent rejection.

Now Try This

c Circle the correct answer.

Dialysis fluid will contain no:

  urea   glucose   water

Dialysis fluid must contain:

  glucose   urea   red blood cells

Dialysis must be carried out three times per:

  week   month   year

During dialysis, blood is taken from a patient's:

  artery   vein   capillary

Urea passes into the dialysis fluid by:

  osmosis   diffusion   active transport

 TOP TIP Some people are born with just one kidney and often never realise!

Homework

10 Explain why dialysis fluid must contain glucose.

11 Explain why dialysis fluid should not contain any urea.

12 Summarise the advantages and disadvantages of dialysis and kidney transplants.

Microbiology

YEAST AND BREWING

- **Anaerobic respiration** in **yeast** involves the incomplete breakdown of glucose molecules.
- This process is called **fermentation**:
  glucose → ethanol + carbon dioxide + energy
- Fermentation is used in **brewing** beer.
- The starch in barley grains is digested by enzymes to form a sugary solution. This is called **malting**.
- Yeast ferment the sugary solution in the absence of oxygen to produce **alcohol**.
- In wine making, yeast ferment the sugar in grape juice to produce alcohol.
- In bread making, the **carbon dioxide** produced by the yeast causes the dough to rise.
- The **ethanol** released is evaporated by the heat of the oven.

Now Try This

a Complete the passage by filling in the missing words.

_____ are single-celled organisms. Yeast can respire aerobically (with _____) or _____ (without oxygen). Anaerobic respiration is called _____. In yeast, fermentation produces _____ _____ and _____. Yeast can be used in _____ beer and _____. Fermentation is also used in making bread. The carbon dioxide produced makes the dough _____.

Homework

1 Explain how fermentation in yeast is used in making bread.
2 Describe how yeast are used to brew beer.
3 Write a paragraph to compare anaerobic respiration in yeast and humans.

BACTERIA AND FERMENTATION

- Some **bacteria** may also carry out **anaerobic respiration**.
- Bacteria may be used to **ferment** the sugar in milk (lactose) to produce **lactic acid**.
- The milk is warmed to make the bacteria grow more quickly.
- Lactic acid causes the milk to solidify into **yoghurt**.
- Bacteria are also used in cheese making.
- A **starter culture** is added to warm milk to produce **curds**, which are more solid than yoghurt.
- The curds are separated from the **whey** (liquid).
- More bacteria and some **moulds** are added to the curds to ripen the cheese.

Now Try This

b Match the following words to their descriptions.

i	Single-celled organisms that produce ethanol.	aerobic
ii	Gas released during respiration.	ethanol
iii	Respiration using oxygen.	anaerobic
iv	Single-celled organisms that produce lactic acid.	yeast
v	Respiration without oxygen.	bacteria
vi	A form of alcohol produced by yeast.	carbon dioxide

Homework

4 Explain how bacteria are used in making yoghurt.
5 Find out what 'live' yoghurt is.
6 Describe the best conditions for growing bacteria.

MICROBES IN INDUSTRY

- **Microorganisms** can be grown on a large scale in industrial **fermenters**.
- Fermenters are large vessels with: a good air supply, a stirrer, a water-cooled jacket, probes to measure pH and temperature and an outlet tap.
- A **nutrient medium** is provided as a source for the organism's respiration.
- The antibiotic **penicillin** is made by growing the *Penicillium* mould in a fermenter.
- **Biogas fuel** can be produced by anaerobic fermentation of various plant products or sewage.
- The *Fusarium* **fungus** is used to produce protein-rich meat substitutes for vegetarians, such as **mycoprotein**.

 The optimum conditions in a fermenter will be different for different microorganisms.

Now Try This

c Match the following functions of a fermenter to the correct parts.

i   To allow the products to be collected.

ii To monitor the pH of the mixture.

iii To monitor the temperature of the mixture.

iv To provide a food source for respiration.

v   To remove heat produced by respiration.

vi To provide oxygen for respiration.

air supply

outlet tap

water-cooled jacket

nutrient medium

temperature probe

pH probe

Homework

7 Explain the function of a stirrer in an industrial fermenter.

8 Explain the function of a water-cooled jacket in an industrial fermenter.

9 What is the purpose of monitoring pH and temperature in a fermenter?

SAFE USE OF MICROBES

- It is important to use pure **cultures** when using **microorganisms**.
- Contaminated cultures may contain microorganisms that are harmful to humans.
- Microorganisms in the laboratory are usually grown in an **agar nutrient medium** containing an energy source, proteins, vitamins and minerals.
- The agar medium is then poured into a Petri dish which is **inoculated** with the required culture.
- Both the nutrient medium and the Petri dish must be **sterilised** before use.
- The **inoculation loop** used to transfer microorganisms is sterilised before use by heating in a blue Bunsen flame.
- The lid of the Petri dish is sealed to prevent other **microorganisms** from entering.
- The use of sterile materials is called '**aseptic technique**'.

 In schools, culture can only be incubated at a temperature of 25 °C.

Now Try This

d Find the following words in this wordsearch.

yeast   bacteria   inoculate
ferment   agar   sterilise

I	I	A	O	O	R	D	E	S
F	N	U	B	Z	X	I	W	T
E	H	O	A	B	P	F	A	E
R	A	I	C	R	A	G	A	R
M	L	V	T	U	L	U	S	I
E	E	T	E	N	L	S	S	L
N	V	B	R	C	N	A	V	I
T	V	C	I	H	G	O	T	S
G	Y	E	A	S	T	N	F	E

Homework

10 Explain why inoculating loops are heated in a blue, rather than a yellow, Bunsen flame.

11 Why may it be necessary to incubate at temperatures above 25 °C in industry?

12 What disadvantages are there of having unwanted microorganisms in a culture?

Periodic table

HISTORY OF THE PERIODIC TABLE

- Newlands and Mendeleev put the first **periodic tables** together. They arranged the **elements** in order of **atomic weight** and put elements with similar properties together in vertical columns called **groups**.
- Not all of the elements were known, so some elements were put in groups where their properties did not fit.
- Mendeleev got round this problem by leaving gaps where he thought an element might be missing.
- **Electrons**, **protons** and **neutrons** were discovered early in the twentieth century. At that time, elements were arranged in order of atomic number, putting elements in the right groups.
- Elements in the same group have the same number of electrons in their highest energy levels (outer shells).

 TOP TIP Check the key on your periodic table. It tells you which number is the atomic number and which is the relative mass.

Now try this

a Place these events in order by putting numbers in the boxes.

- ☐ Atomic numbers assigned to the elements.
- ☐ Elements organised in order of atomic weight.
- ☐ Mendeleev left gaps for undiscovered elements.
- ☐ Protons, electrons and neutrons discovered.
- ☐ Atomic weights of the known elements worked out.
- ☐ Elements arranged in atomic number order.
- 7 Scientists noted that the group number equalled the outer number of electrons

Homework

1 How are the elements in your periodic table organised?

2 Find out about John Newlands or Dmitri Mendeleev and produce a leaflet about **one** of them.

GROUP 1 – THE ALKALI METALS

- **Group 1** elements are called the **alkali metals** because they react with water to make alkalis (**metal hydroxides**) and hydrogen gas.
- Group 1 metals have low densities and three of them (Li, Na and K) float on water.
- When they react with non-metals they make white **ionic solids** which dissolve in water to make colourless solutions.
- There is just one electron in their highest energy level and when they lose this they form ions with a charge of +1.
- As you go down group 1 the elements become more reactive because it becomes easier to lose the electrons in their highest energy level.
- Going down group 1, melting points decrease.

Now try this

b Tick the boxes that show the properties of alkali metals.

i	Low density	☐
ii	React with water making oxygen	☐
iii	React with oxygen making white solid	☐
iv	Become less reactive down the group	☐
v	Increase in reactivity down the group	☐
vi	Have ions with a charge of +1	☐
vii	Melting point increases down the group	☐
viii	React with water forming hydroxides which dissolve in water	☐

Homework

3 Why are the elements in group 1 known as the alkali metals?

4 Draw cartoon diagrams of Li, Na and K which give an indication of how reactive they are.

GROUP 7 – THE HALOGENS

- These elements form molecules made of pairs of atoms, for example Cl_2.
- They have coloured vapours.
- They react with metals forming **ionic compounds** containing **halide ions** which have charge of –1.
- They also react with non-metals to form **molecular compounds**.
- As you go down the group, they decrease in reactivity because it becomes harder to attract an electron into their highest energy level.
- As you go down the group, the melting and boiling points increase.
- A more reactive **halogen** (like chlorine) can **displace** a less reactive halogen (like bromine) from its aqueous solution.

| F |
| Cl |
| Br |
| I |
| At |

Less reactive
Increase in melting and boiling point

Now try this

c Tick the boxes that show properties of halogens.

i   Form ionic compounds with metals ☐

ii Form molecules when they react with metals ☐

iii Increase in reactivity going down the group ☐

iv Have coloured vapours ☐

v   Have ions with a charge of –1 called halides ☐

vi Melting point increases going down the group ☐

vii Become less reactive going down the group ☐

viii Form diatomic molecules ☐

Homework

5 Draw cartoon diagrams of atoms of Cl, Br and I which indicate their state and colour.

6 Which is the most reactive halogen?

7 Describe an experiment you could do to show that chlorine is more reactive than bromine.

THE TRANSITION ELEMENTS

- These metals lie between **group 2** and **group 3** of the periodic table.
- Compared to group 1 metals, **transition metals**:
  - are much denser
  - are stronger and harder
  - are much less reactive
  - have higher melting points (except mercury)
- Transition elements have ions with different charges, for example iron has Fe^{2+} and Fe^{3+} ions.
- Transition elements have special properties because a lower energy level is being filled.
- This is because the third energy level can actually hold up to 18 electrons once 2 electrons have gone into the fourth energy level.
- Transition elements form many coloured compounds.
- Transition elements (and their compounds) make useful **catalysts**.

Now try this

d Tick the boxes that show properties of transition metals.

i   Form coloured compounds ☐

ii Can float on water ☐

iii Are soft ☐

iv Are dense ☐

v   Are strong ☐

vi Make good catalysts ☐

vii Are unreactive ☐

Homework

8   Draw up a table to compare the properties of the group 1 metals and transition metals.

9   Using iron as an example, describe the properties of transition metals.

10 Explain why the transition metals have special properties.

Acids and alkalis

HISTORY OF ACIDS AND ALKALIS

- In 1887 a Swedish chemist, Arrhenius, first suggested that **acid** solutions contained $H^+_{(aq)}$ ions.
- Other chemists said that an H^+ was just a proton and that it was too small to exist, so it took some time for the work of Arrhenius to be accepted.
- Much later in 1923, Brönsted (a Swede) and Lowry (an Englishman) proposed that an acid is a **proton donor** and a **base** is a **proton acceptor**.
- This was more acceptable as it did not require a tiny proton to have a separate existence.
- It also meant that an acid could not behave as an acid on its own. It could only act as an acid if it was put with a base that could accept its protons.

Now try this

a Place these events in the correct order to show how ideas about acids developed.

☐ They say that a proton cannot possibly exist on its own.

☐ Other scientists disagree with Arrhenius.

☐ You learn that an acid cannot donate its protons unless a base is present to accept them.

☐ Arrhenius states that acids make H^+ in solution.

☐ Brönsted and Lowry suggest that an acid is able to donate a proton and a base can accept a proton.

Homework

1 Use the Internet to find pictures of Arrhenius, Lowry and Brönsted and print them out.
2 Use these to create a cartoon strip showing a conversation they might have had about acids.
3 Explain why an acid cannot behave as an acid on its own.

ACIDS AND ALKALIS

- An **acid** is a **proton donor**. HCl is an acid because it can donate H^+ ions.
- A hydrogen ion, H^+, is a proton.
- A **base** is a **proton acceptor**. NaOH is a base because the OH^- can accept an H^+ ion.
- Water normally has to be present for a substance to act as a base or an acid.
- When acids are placed in water, H^+ ions are produced. They are hydrated and are shown as $H^+_{(aq)}$.
- Alkalis produce hydrated OH^- ions in aqueous solution. These are written as $OH^-_{(aq)}$.

Now try this

b Which of the following statements about bases are true? Put a tick by the correct statements.

i Bases cannot be bases all on their own. ☐

ii Ammonia can act as a base. ☐

iii Bases are proton donors. ☐

iv Bases are proton acceptors. ☐

v The oxides and hydroxides of metals are bases. ☐

vi Bases produce $OH^+_{(aq)}$ in aqueous solution. ☐

vii All bases produce $OH^-_{(aq)}$ in aqueous solution. ☐

Homework

4 Look at the labels on cans and bottles around your house. List all of the acids you can find.
5 Explain why HCl dissolved in petrol does not behave as an acid.
6 Explain why NH_3 solution acts as an alkali.

STRONG AND WEAK ACIDS

- When an acid splits up in water and forms $H^+_{(aq)}$, we say it has **dissociated**.
- An acid that fully dissociates is called a **strong acid**, for example hydrochloric, sulfuric and nitric acid.
- A **weak acid** is one that only partly dissociates, for example citric, ethanoic and carbonic acids.
- **Strong alkalis** fully dissociate in water and include sodium and potassium hydroxide.
- A **weak alkali** that only partially dissociates is ammonia.
- We carry out **titrations** to find the volumes of acids and alkalis that just **neutralise** each other.

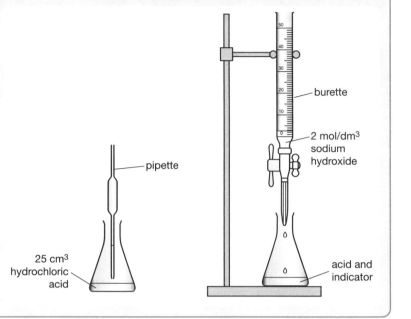

pipette

25 cm³ hydrochloric acid

burette

2 mol/dm³ sodium hydroxide

acid and indicator

Homework

7   Explain what you understand by the term 'dissociation' when talking about an acid.

8   Draw up a table to list weak and strong acids.

TITRATIONS

- You must choose the correct **indicator** for a **titration**:
  - strong acid with strong alkali → any acid–base indicator
  - strong acid with weak alkali → methyl orange indicator
  - weak acid with strong alkali → phenolphthalein
- In the diagram above, the sodium hydroxide is added to the acid until the indicator shows it has become **neutral**.
- The equation for this titration is:
  HCl + NaOH → NaCl + H_2O.
- The volume of NaOH used (titre) is measured from the **burette**.
- The titration is repeated and an average titre found.
- The number of moles of NaOH is calculated using the equation: moles = concentration × volume
- The equation is used to find the ratio of HCl : NaOH. It is a 1 : 1 ratio. This tells us how many moles of acid were used.
- Knowing the volume of acid and the **moles** of acid you can now calculate the **concentration** of the acid.

Now try this

c   Three titrations using the solutions in the diagram above were carried out and the following titres obtained: 18.00 cm³, 17.80 cm³ and 18.20 cm³

Circle the correct answers below.

i   Average titre in cm³

    17.80   18.10   18.00

ii   Moles of NaOH used

    0.036   0.0036   0.36

iii   Moles of HCl used

    0.36   0.072   0.036

iv   Concentration of acid in mol/dm³

    1.44   1.88   2.44

TOP TIP When finding moles in solution, the volume must be given in dm³. 1 dm³ is equal to 1000 cm³. To convert cm³ to dm³ you must divide by 1000.

Homework

9   Calculate the number of moles of HCl in 50 cm³ of $HCl_{(aq)}$ with a concentration of 2 mol/dm³.

10   What volume of 1 mol/dm³ NaOH is needed to just neutralise this amount of acid?

Water

WATER IS AN EXCELLENT SOLVENT

- **Water** on the Earth is constantly being **recycled**. Water in lakes, rivers and oceans is **evaporated** and forms **water vapour**. This rises and cools, making it **condense**, and clouds form. Water droplets in the clouds join up and the water falls as rain.
- Many gases **dissolve** in water. The **solubility** of gases in water decreases as the temperature increases.
- If we dissolve carbon dioxide in water under pressure we make fizzy water. This is known as **carbonated water**.
- When we release the lid on fizzy water, the pressure is reduced and the gas escapes from the water.
- **Dissolved oxygen** in water is essential for aquatic life.
- As the temperature of water increases, the amount of dissolved oxygen it can hold decreases.

Now try this

a Number the steps below to explain how water from my garden pond ends up as a puddle in your garden.

- ☐ Water droplets join together and fall as rain in your garden.
- ☐ Sunshine warms up the water in my pond.
- ☐ Water vapour is formed.
- ☐ The water vapour rises and cools.
- ☐ The water evaporates.
- ☐ Clouds form.

Homework

1 Draw a labelled diagram to show the water cycle.
2 Explain why lemonade feels fizzy on your tongue.
3 Explain why fish may die if the water in their tank becomes too hot.

SOLUBILITY

- Most **ionic compounds dissolve** in water. Most **covalent substances** do not dissolve in water.
- The **solubility** of a substance is given in grams of **solute** per 100 grams of water at that temperature.
- The solubility of solids generally increases when the temperature is raised.
- A **saturated solution** is one that cannot dissolve any more solute at a given temperature.
- If a hot saturated solution is cooled down then solid comes out of the solution.

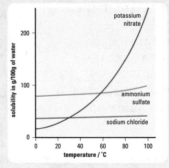

Now try this

b Refer to the graph on the left and answer these questions.

Which is the most soluble solid at 20 °C? _____

Which is the least soluble solid at 100 °C? _____

Which is the most soluble solid at 90 °C? _____

Which solid could dissolve about 100 g in 200 g water at 40 °C? _____

Homework

4 Explain why sodium chloride dissolves in water but a hydrocarbon like petrol does not.
5 Explain what happens to the solubility of sodium chloride as the temperature decreases.
6 Describe what you would see if a saturated solution of sodium chloride is allowed to cool.

HARDNESS IN WATER

- **Hard water** contains dissolved compounds of **magnesium** and **calcium**.
- These compounds get into the water from rocks which the water passes through.
- Hard water reacts with soap to form **scum**. This means more soap is needed to get a **lather** and costs are therefore increased.
- Another problem with hard water is that when heated, it produces **scale** in kettles and boilers and efficiency is therefore reduced.
- Hard water has some good points. Calcium compounds are good for our health.
- Calcium and magnesium can be removed by adding sodium carbonate, which causes them to **precipitate out**.
- Passing the water through an **ion exchange column** removes the Ca^{2+} and Mg^{2+} ions and replaces them with sodium or hydrogen ions.

Soft water gives a good lather.

Now try this

c Answer the following questions with **soft** or **hard**.

Water that is difficult to get a lather with. _____

Water that is good for your health. _____

Water containing Ca^{2+} and Mg^{2+}. _____

Water that does not make a scum. _____

Water that does not form scale in boilers. _____

Homework

7 Name **two** ions that cause hardness in water. How do they get there?

8 What are the good and bad points about soft water?

9 Draw labelled diagrams to show **two** ways in which hard water can be softened.

MAKING WATER SAFE

- Levels of **dissolved solids** and **microorganisms** in drinking water should be low.
- Water supplies are treated by passing them through **filter beds** which remove solids.
- Water supplies are then **sterilised** using **chlorine**.
- Water **filters** can contain the elements **carbon** and **silver**, as well as **ion exchange resins**.
- Together, these remove the dissolved salts and may improve quality and taste.
- Pure water without any dissolved solids can be made by distillation.

Now try this

d Circle the correct answers.

i Filter beds remove

    solids   microorganisms   dissolved solids

ii Ion exchange columns remove

    solids   microorganisms   dissolved solids

iii Distillation is done to remove

    solids   microorganisms   dissolved solids

iv Chlorine treatment removes

    solids   microorganisms   dissolved solids

 TOP TIP Distillation involves evaporating water and then condensing it. Dissolved solids are left behind as the water evaporates.

Homework

10 Explain why our water is treated with chlorine.

11 How do water filters work?

12 Draw a diagram to show the apparatus you would need to get pure water from seawater.

Energy changes in chemical reactions

MEASURING ENERGY CHANGES

- The relative amount of energy released when substances are burnt can be compared by using the energy to heat water in a glass or metal container.
- This method is called **calorimetry**.
- The substance that gives out the most energy will increase the water's temperature the most.
- To measure the energy produced when a solid and a solution react can be found by carrying out the reaction in an insulated container and measuring the temperature change.
- The same method can be used to measure the energy given out when an acid and an alkali react (neutralisation).

 TOP TIP Energy is normally measured in joules.

Now try this

a Number the list below to show the correct order in which an experiment must be carried out to compare the energy output of fuels A and B.

☐	20 cm^3 of water is placed in a beaker and its temperature measured.
7	The experiment is repeated with fuel B using 20 cm^3 of fresh water.
1	A spirit burner is filled with fuel A then weighed.
☐	The temperature change is divided by the mass of fuel burnt.
☐	When the temperature reaches 80 °C the burner is removed and reweighed.
☐	The beaker is placed above the spirit burner.
☐	The burner is lit and the heat from the burning fuel is used to heat the water.

Homework

1. Draw a diagram to show how you could compare the energy when two fuels are burnt.
2. What will happen to the temperature when this reaction occurs: $H^+_{(aq)} + OH^-_{(aq)} \rightarrow H_2O_{(l)}$.
3. Heat is needed to decompose calcium carbonate. Is the reaction endothermic or exothermic?

ENERGY IN FOOD

- **Food labels** show the amount of energy contained in foods.
- Some labels give the energy content in **calories**. One calorie is equal to 4.2 joules.
- Different foods contain different amounts of energy.
- Fats, oils and carbohydrates are foods which contain a lot of energy.
- If you eat food that gives your body more energy than it needs, your body stores it as **fat**.
- Eating too much food containing these food groups can lead to **obesity**.

Now try this

b Complete these sentences by filling in the missing words.

A bag of crisps states that it contains 260 kJ (kilojoules) of _____. This is the same as 1092 _____. The food groups which are in the packet are likely to be _____ and _____. Both of these food groups provide a lot of energy and if a person eats too much of these foods they may become _____.

Homework

4. Look through the food with labels on in your kitchen. Which food gives the most energy?
5. Draw a picture to show **six** items an obese person should not eat too much of.
6. A label says a food gives 80 calories per 100 g. How many joules would there be in 20 g?

WHAT CAUSES ENERGY CHANGES?

- Energy is taken in to break bonds in reactants. Bond breaking is endothermic. This is the **activation energy**. When the products form, bonds are made and this gives out energy. Bond forming is **exothermic**.

- Some reactions are exothermic. This means that overall they give out energy. For example, **combustion** and **respiration**.

- Some reactions take in energy overall. These reactions are endothermic. For example, **thermal decomposition** of calcium carbonate. In endothermic reactions, more energy is taken in when bonds are broken in the reactants than is given out when bonds form in the products.

- These energy changes can be shown on **energy level diagrams**.

- **Catalysts** lower the activation energy of a reaction making it more likely to happen.

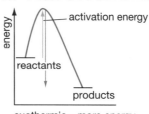

exothermic – more energy given out than taken in

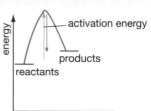

endothermic – less energy given out than taken in

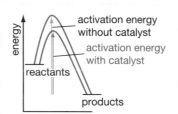

Homework

7 Draw an energy level diagram for an endothermic reaction without a catalyst.

8 In terms of bonding, explain why a particular reaction is exothermic.

9 Explain how a catalyst speeds up a reaction.

CALCULATING ENERGY CHANGES

- Calculate the energy needed to break the bonds in the reactants:
  $4 \times$ C-H $= 4 \times 412 = 1648$ kJ $2 \times$ O=O $= 2 \times 496 = 992$ kJ
  Total energy needed = _____ kJ

- Calculate the energy given out when bonds form in the products:
  $4 \times$ O-H $= 4 \times 463 = 1852$ kJ $2 \times$ C=O $= 2 \times 743 = 1486$ kJ
  Total energy given out = _____ kJ

- Find the difference between the energy taken in and that given out. This is the energy change.
  3338 kJ – 2640 kJ = _____ kJ overall

- Work out if it is exothermic or endothermic. More energy is given out in bond forming than taken in during bond breaking so the reaction is _____ overall.

Now try this

c Follow the step by step instructions on the left, filling in the gaps, to find out the overall energy change when methane burns. Use the bond energy data provided below.

Bond energies in kJ

C—H = 412   C—O = 463
O=O = 496   C=O = 743

$$\begin{array}{c} H \\ | \\ H-C-H \\ | \\ H \end{array} + 2O{=}O \rightarrow 2H{-}O{-}H + O{=}C{=}O$$

Homework

10 On the Internet go to: http://www.bbc.co.uk/schools/gcsebitesize/chemistry/chemicalreactions and then select 'Energy changes in reactions'. Work through the revision section and then try the test.

Chemical analysis

TESTS FOR METAL IONS

- **Flame tests** are used to test for some metals.

Lithium Li^+ – crimson red	Barium Ba^{2+} – green
Potassium K^+ – lilac	Calcium Ca^{2+} – brick red
Sodium Na^+ – orange/yellow	

- **Sodium hydroxide** solution can be added to detect some metal ions.

Copper(II)	Cu^{2+}	Forms a blue **precipitate** (ppt)
Iron(II)	Fe^{2+}	Forms a dull green ppt
Iron(III)	Fe^{3+}	Forms a rusty ppt
Aluminium	Al^{3+}	Forms a white ppt which redissolves in excess NaOH
Calcium	Ca^{2+}	Forms a white ppt
Magnesium	Mg^{2+}	Forms a white ppt
Ammonium	NH_4^+	Makes NH_3 gas which turns damp red litmus blue

- Green copper carbonate **decomposes** on heating to form black copper oxide.
- Zinc carbonate decomposes on heating to form zinc oxide, which is yellow when hot, white when cold.

Now try this

a Circle the correct answer.

  i Gives a blue ppt with NaOH:
  Cu^{2+} Al^{3+} Fe^{3+}

  ii Has a crimson red flame colour:
  Ca^{2+} NH_4^+ Li^+

  iii Forms a white ppt with NaOH that redissolves in excess:
  Al^{3+} Ba^{2+} Na^+

  iv Has an orange/yellow flame colour:
  Na^+ Ba^{2+} K^+

  v Forms a brown ppt with NaOH:
  Fe^{3+} Mg^{2+} Fe^{2+}

 TOP TIP A precipitate (ppt) is a solid that forms when two solutions are mixed.

Homework

1   Describe how you would prove a solution contains dissolved copper ions.

2   If a white solid is heated and it turns yellow but goes white again on cooling, what is it?

TESTING FOR NEGATIVE IONS

- Adding dilute hydrochloric acid to any carbonate (CO_3^{2-}) releases carbon dioxide gas.
- We can test for the **halide ions** (Cl^-, Br^-, I^-) by adding dilute nitric acid followed by silver nitrate solution.
- Cl^- ions give a white ppt, Br^- ions a cream ppt and I^- ions a yellow ppt.
- **Sulfate ions** (SO_4^{2-}) can be identified by adding hydrochloric acid followed by barium chloride solution. A white ppt forms.
- To test for **nitrate ions** we add some aluminium powder and sodium hydroxide and warm it. This gives ammonia gas.

Now try this

b Match the following results with the correct conclusions.

Result	Conclusion
i Cream ppt with nitric acid and silver nitrate	iodide ion
ii White ppt with hydrochloric acid and barium chloride	carbonate ion
iii Yellow ppt with nitric acid and silver nitrate	bromide ion
iv Bubbles when HCl (aq) added and gas turns limewater milky	sulfate ion

Homework

3   Make a poster to show tests for **a)** nitrates **b)** carbonates and **c)** halides. On the poster, make sure you show what result you would get in each case.

4   Add a diagram to the poster to show how you test for carbon dioxide gas and ammonia.

ORGANIC ANALYSIS

- You can tell if you have an **organic compound** as it will char (go black) when heated in air.
- You can see if an organic compound is **unsaturated** by adding bromine water.
- You can find the **empirical formula** of an organic compound by burning a known mass of it and finding the mass of products.

Organic material (containing carbon) chars when heated.

Now try this

c Complete these sentences by filling in the missing words.

A compound is heated and it chars. This tells us the substance is _____. When it is mixed with bromine water the bromine water turns from brown to _____, which tells us that the molecule is _____ (it contains a _____ bond).

Homework

5 What would happen to sugar if it was heated in a test tube?

6 What would you see if the following were shaken with bromine water **a)** methane **b)** ethene?

7 Find out and explain what the word 'empirical' means.

MODERN INSTRUMENTAL METHODS

- Elements and compounds can be detected and identified using different **instruments**.
- This is more accurate, more sensitive and much faster than other methods.
- Smaller amounts of sample are needed using these modern instruments.
- **Atomic absorption spectroscopy** is used in the steel industry to identify particular elements present and their percentage.
- **Mass spectrometers** can be used to identify the presence of particular elements or compounds.
- **Gas-liquid chromatography** can be used to separate out the different compounds in a mixture.
- **Infrared spectroscopy** and **nuclear magnetic resonance spectroscopy** are used to identify organic compounds.
- **Ultraviolet spectroscopy** is another technique used to identify compounds.

Now try this

d Use the letters to show the uses and characteristics of each technique. The first one has been done for you.

A = **mass spectroscopy**
B = **gas-liquid chromatography**
C = **atomic absorption spectroscopy**
D = **infrared spectroscopy**

i Is very quick and accurate	A, B, C and D
ii To separate a number of organic compounds	_____
iii To identify elements in the steel industry	_____
iv Aided by the development of technology	_____
v Only needs small amounts of sample	_____
vi Uses mass of particles to identify elements	_____

Homework

8 What are the advantages of modern instruments in chemical analysis?

9 Draw up a table to show the different analytical instruments and what they are useful for.

10 Search the Internet and print out a mass spectrum for any organic compound you have heard of.

Turning and circles

TURNING EFFECTS

- The **turning effect** of a **force** about a point is called the **moment** of the force.
- The turning effect of a force about a **pivot** is given by:

    moment (Nm) = force (N) × perpendicular distance of force from the pivot (m)

- The **centre-of-mass** of an object is a point where the entire mass appears to be concentrated.
- The centre-of-mass of a symmetrical body is along its axis of symmetry.
- For a body in **equilibrium**, the net force and the net moment are both equal to zero.
- **Principle of moments**: For a body in equilibrium, the sum of the clockwise moments about a point is equal to the sum of the anticlockwise moments about that point.
- An object will topple if the line of action of its weight falls outside the base of the body.

Now try this

a Cross out the incorrect word in each sentence, leaving the correct word.

Moment of a force depends on distance and the size of the **force/mass**.

If the net moment is zero, then an object **will/will not** rotate.

The centre-of-mass of a ball is at its **base/centre**.

Homework

1 Make a list of all the key definitions and units in this section.
2 Draw some objects with their centre-of-masses clearly shown.
3 In terms of stability, explain why some monkeys have long tails.

MOVING IN A CIRCLE

- An object moving in a circle with a constant speed will have a changing **velocity**.
- An object moving in a circle has **acceleration** acting towards the centre of the circle. The acceleration is known as **centripetal acceleration**.
- The **resultant force** causing the centripetal acceleration is known as the **centripetal force**.
- The direction of the centripetal force is also towards the centre of the circle.
- The centripetal force is given by:

    centripetal force (N) = mass (kg) × centripetal acceleration (m/s²)

- The centripetal force is:
  - directly proportional to the mass of the object
  - directly proportional to the speed² of the object
  - inversely proportional to the radius.
- The centripetal force acting on an object is given by:

    $$\text{centripetal force} = \frac{(\text{mass of object} \times \text{speed}^2)}{\text{radius}}$$

Now try this

b Place a tick (✓) at the end of each statement if it is correct.

i Velocity and speed are the same. ☐

ii The centripetal force and acceleration are in the same direction. ☐

iii Whirling a stone at the end of a string faster will increase the tension in the string. ☐

4 Draw a mind map for this section.

5 In your own words, describe the factors that affect the size of the centripetal force on an object moving in a circle.

6 Make a list of objects that move in a circle.

PLANETS AND SATELLITES

- **Gravitational force** keeps a **satellite** (natural or artificial) or a planet in **orbit**.
- Gravitational force is an attractive force.
- Gravitational force between two bodies increases when the masses of the bodies are bigger and it decreases when the separation between the bodies is greater.
- The orbits of the planets around the Sun are **elliptical** ('squashed circles').
- Gravitational force provides the centripetal force that allows a planet or a satellite to maintain a circular orbit.
- A planet closer to the Sun has a shorter **orbital period** because the gravitational force of the Sun is stronger.
- A **geostationary satellite** orbits the Earth once every 24 hours. It remains in a fixed position above the Earth.
- The orbital period of an artificial satellite increases with increasing height from the Earth's surface.
- **Communication satellites** are often in geostationary orbit above the equator.
- **Monitoring satellites** have low polar **orbits**.

Now try this

c Cross out the incorrect word in each sentence, leaving the correct word.

Planets move round the Sun because of **gravitational/magnetic** force.

The gravitational force between objects is always **repulsive/attractive**.

A satellite orbits the **Sun/planets**.

Mercury has a very short orbital period because its distance from the Sun is **small/large**.

7 Describe the nature of gravitational force between the Sun and the planets in our Solar System.

8 Describe the motion of a geostationary satellite and its practical uses.

9 Use the Internet to research and write about the planet in our Solar System with the most elliptical orbit.

Light and sound

MIRRORS AND LENSES

- **magnification** = $\dfrac{\text{image height}}{\text{object height}}$
- The **image** produced by a **plane mirror** is virtual, upright, the same size as the object, the same distance behind the mirror as the distance of the object from the mirror and laterally inverted.
- The image produced by a **convex** (diverging) mirror is always virtual, upright and diminished.
- Parallel rays of light are reflected by a **concave mirror** and pass through the **focal point (focus)**.
- The nature of the image produced by a **concave** (converging) mirror depends on the position of the object.
- A **convex lens** is a converging lens. It is thicker at its centre.
- The bending of light as it travels from one medium into another is called **refraction**.
- Refraction takes place because the speed of light changes as it travels from one medium into another.
- Parallel rays of light passing through a convex lens pass through the focal point (focus).
- The **focal length** of a lens is the distance between the lens and the focus.
- Projectors and cameras produce **real images**, which can be formed on a screen.
- Real images formed by a convex lens are always inverted.
- A convex lens can be used as a magnifying glass when the object is between the lens and the focus. The image is virtual, upright and magnified.

Homework

1 Make a list of instruments or devices that use a lens.
2 Draw a ray diagram to show the focal point (focus) and focal length of a convex lens.
3 Draw a ray diagram for an object placed at a distance of one and a half times the focal length from the centre of a concave mirror. Describe the properties of the image.

SOUND

See page 34 Panel 1, 'Understanding waves' for definitions of wavelength and frequency.

- The **amplitude** of a wave is the maximum distance of a particle from its normal (or equilibrium) position.
- Sound is a **longitudinal wave**. The particles vibrate parallel to the direction in which the wave travels.
- Sound cannot travel through a vacuum because there are no particles.
- The human ear can detect sound in the **frequency range** 20 Hz to 20 000 Hz.
- Increasing the frequency of sound increases the **pitch** of the note.
- Increasing the amplitude of sound increases the **loudness**.
- The quality of sound depends on the **waveform**. A perfect pitch is produced by a **sinusoidal signal**.

Now try this

a Find the following key words in this wordsearch.

ear	note	pitch
loudness	hertz	vacuum

N	E	E	T	U	V	H	Z
P	V	E	L	N	P	E	L
I	P	A	Z	V	O	R	P
T	U	R	C	N	O	T	E
C	P	N	L	U	V	Z	O
H	K	A	V	A	U	L	E
T	E	E	E	L	Z	M	N
S	S	E	N	D	U	O	L

Homework

4 Draw a mind map for sound.

5 With the help of suitable diagrams, write a short paragraph on pitch and loudness.

6 Make a list of the differences between sound and light.

ULTRASOUND

- **Ultrasound** has frequencies higher than 20 000 Hz and cannot be heard by humans.
- Ultrasound creates regions of high pressure called **compressions** and regions of low pressure called **rarefactions**.
- Ultrasound is used for 'seeing' inside our bodies without surgery.
- **Ultrasound scans** are used to check the condition of foetuses in pregnant women and breaking down kidney stones.
- Ultrasound is partially reflected by different layers of tissues.
- Unlike **X-ray scans**, ultrasound scans can be used to produce images of soft tissues and they do not damage living cells.
- Ultrasound is used in industry for cleaning.

Now try this

b Match the statements on the left-hand side with the correct terms on the right-hand side.

i What is the unit of frequency?   kidney

ii What type of wave is ultrasound?   longitudinal

iii What type of stones can ultrasound break down?   hertz

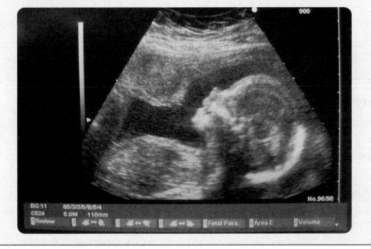

Homework

7 In your own words describe amplitude, frequency and wavelength of an ultrasound.

8 Describe some of the applications of ultrasound.

9 Use a search engine to search for some images of ultrasound scans.

Motors, generators and stars

MOTORS

- A **current-carrying wire** is surrounded by a **magnetic field**. The magnetic field lines are concentric circles round the wire.
- A current-carrying wire placed in a magnetic field experiences a **force**.
- The force experienced by the wire increases when the strength of the magnetic field is increased or when the current in the wire is increased.
- The current-carrying wire does not experience any force when the wire is parallel to the magnetic field.
- A simple **motor** has a rectangular frame of wire that is placed in a magnetic field. The opposite limbs of the frame experience equal and opposite forces and this causes the frame to rotate.

Now try this

a Circle the items required to make an electric motor.

battery

resistor

wire frame

lamp

magnet

clock

Homework

1 Draw the magnetic field pattern for a current-carrying wire. Describe how the field pattern changes when the current is increased and when the current is reversed.
2 Research and write about how a simple motor works off a battery.
3 Describe how you can increase the speed of a motor.

GENERATORS

See page 32 Panel 1 on generating electricity.

- A **potential difference** is induced across the ends of a wire when it 'cuts' a **magnetic field**.
- A potential difference will also be induced when a moving magnetic field 'cuts' a stationary wire.
- A **current** will be induced in the wire if it forms a complete circuit.
- The size of the induced potential difference increases when:
  - the speed of movement is increased
  - the strength of the magnetic field is increased
  - the number of turns are increased
  - the area of the coil or circuit is larger.

Now try this

b Circle the items that affect the size of the induced potential difference in a generator.

strength of magnetic field

current

speed of rotation

type of wire

number of turns

type of battery

Homework

4 Research and write about AC generators. Draw a clearly labelled diagram and describe the purpose of the slip rings and carbon brushes.
5 Make a list of places where AC generators are used.
6 Describe how you can increase the induced potential difference from a generator.

TRANSFORMERS

See page 31 Panel 3 on electricity .

- A **transformer** consists of a **primary coil** (input) and a **secondary coil** (output). Both coils are wound onto an **iron core**.
- A changing **current** in the primary coil produces a changing **magnetic field** in the iron core. This changing field links the secondary coil and so a **potential difference** is induced in the secondary coil.
- **Turn-ratio** equation:

$$\frac{\text{pd across primary}}{\text{pd across secondary}} = \frac{\text{number of turns on primary}}{\text{number of turns on secondary}}$$

- In a **step-up transformer**, the number of turns on the secondary coil is more than that on the primary coil and this induces a potential difference across the secondary coil that is larger than the input potential difference.
- In a **step-down transformer**, the number of turns on the secondary coil is fewer than that on the primary coil and this induces a potential difference across the secondary coil that is smaller than the input potential difference.

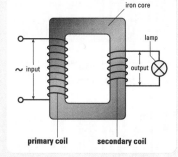

iron core, *lamp*, *~ input*, *output*, *primary coil*, *secondary coil*

Now try this

c Circle the items required to make a transformer.

wire

iron ring

battery

brushes

rubber ring

compass

alternating current supply

Homework

7 In your own words describe how a transformer works.

8 Research and write about how transformers are used by power stations and the National Grid.

HISTORY OF STARS

See pages 40-41 Panels 2 and 3 on the Universe .

- All **stars** have been created from interstellar gas and dust particles.
- Our **Sun** is one of millions of stars in our **galaxy** the Milky Way.
- A star has a stable size because of the balance between **gravitational pressure** and **radiation pressure**.
- A star similar to the Sun will go through the following cycle:
    star → red giant → planetary nebula and white dwarf
- A star much more massive than our Sun will follow the cycle:
    star → red giant → supernova and neutron star or black hole
- The early **Universe** contained hydrogen but now it also contains different elements.
- These elements were created in the interiors of stars from **nuclear fusion reactions**. The elements have been distributed throughout the Universe by **supernova** (exploding stars).

Now try this

d Write the key words from this section starting with the following letters.

B_____

D_____

E_____

G_____

H_____

S_____

U_____

Homework

9   Use the Internet to find out about the composition of a star like our Sun.

10 According to a student, we are all 'star dust'. Write a short paragraph in support of this statement.

Exam-style questions

Biology B1a and B1b

1 The table shows some effects of smoking on the body. Match the words **A**, **B**, **C** and **D** with the statements **1–4** in the table.

A Carbon monoxide   **B** Tar
C Nicotine   **D** Smoke particles   [1]

	Effect on the body
1	reduces the amount of oxygen carried in the blood
2	causes coughing
3	causes cancer
4	is addictive

2 Different organs in the body contain different kinds of receptors. Match the parts of the body **A**, **B**, **C** and **D** with the statements **1–4** in the table.

A Ears   **B** Eyes   **C** Skin   **D** Nose   [1]

	Receptors
1	contains receptors for temperature and pressure
2	contains sound and balance receptors
3	contains light receptors
4	contains receptors for chemicals

3 The passage below describes the sequence of events that occur during a reflex action. Match the words **A**, **B**, **C** and **D** with the spaces **1–4** in the sentences.

A effector   **B** motor neurone
C sensory neurone   **D** receptors   [1]

Stimuli are detected by ___1___ in the sense organs. Nerve impulses are carried to the CNS by a ___2___. A ___3___ carries the nerve impulse back to the ___4___ to bring about a response.

4 Below are some data collected to show the average number of different lichen species growing on tree barks at different distances from a city centre.

Distance from city centre (km)	Average number of lichen species in given area
8	0
12	5
16	10
20	25
24	40
32	40

Which of the following statements about the data in the table is true?

A Lichens only grow in the city centre.

B The number of lichen species increases as you move out of the city centre.

C The number of lichen species decreases as you move out of the city centre.

D The distance from the city centre does not affect the number of lichen species.   [1]

5 The Earth's climate is affected by human activities. Match the words **A**, **B**, **C** and **D** to the spaces **1–4** in the sentences below.

A carbon dioxide   **B** deforestation
C fossil fuels   **D** global warming

When humans burn ___1___ large amounts of ___2___ are released into the atmosphere. ___3___ also increases the amount of carbon dioxide in the atmosphere. An increased amount of carbon dioxide in the atmosphere causes ___4___.   [1]

6 Members of the same family often look like each other. Match the words **A**, **B**, **C** and **D** to the spaces **1–4** in the sentences below.

A nucleus   **B** DNA
C genes   **D** chromosomes

Inherited characteristics are controlled by ___1___. Genes are found in the ___2___ of cells. The genes are made from a chemical called ___3___. This is packaged into structures called ___4___.

7 a Write down two harmful substances found in tobacco smoke.   [2]

    b Describe the effect of one of these substances on the body.   [1]

                               [Total 3 marks]

8 Explain why it is not a good idea to drive after drinking alcohol.   [2]

9 Explain how deforestation may contribute to global warming.   [4]

10 Describe three ways in which a limestone quarry might have a negative impact on the environment.   [3]

11 Describe two reasons why a species may become extinct.   [2]

Chemistry C1a and C1b

1 Match the words **A**, **B**, **C** and **D** with the spaces **1–4** in the sentences.

A atom   **B** nucleus
C electrons   **D** elements

All atoms have a central ___**1**___ which is surrounded by ___**2**___. There are about 100 different ___**3**___, each of which is made of one type of ___**4**___ only.   [1]

2 Match the words **A**, **B**, **C**, and **D** with the labels **1–4** on the diagram.

A polymerisation   **B** fractional distillation
C combustion   **D** cracking   [1]

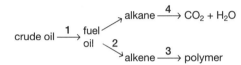

3 Which of these is NOT a use for limestone?

A Reducing copper oxide to obtain copper

B Making slaked lime for neutralising acidity in soils

C Making glass

D Making mortar for use in building   [1]

4 Pick the correct ending to this statement.

Vegetable oils are unsaturated...

A this means that all of the carbon–carbon bonds are single bonds.

B this means they contain carbon–carbon bonds like those in ethene.

C you can show this by reacting them with a group 1 metal.

D they cannot be hardened to make margarine.   [1]

5 Pick the correct ending to this statement.

The Earth's atmosphere...

A is rather like the atmospheres of Jupiter and Mars today.

B has much less carbon dioxide now than it did originally.

C used to contain large amounts of ammonia and oxygen.

D has shown a decrease in carbon dioxide levels over the past 100 years.   [1]

6 Ores are obtained by quarrying.

a Explain what you understand by the term 'ore'. [1]

b Not everyone would think that having a quarry near them was a bad idea. Give one advantage of having a quarry nearby and two disadvantages.   [3]

[Total 4 marks]

7 Iron oxide is reduced to iron in a blast furnace. The iron made in this way has 4 % impurities.

a What problem do these impurities cause if left in the iron?   [1]

b Most iron is made into alloys. What is an alloy? [1]

c What is the advantage of the alloy 'high carbon steel'?   [1]

[Total 3 marks]

8 **a** Name two gases made when a pure hydrocarbon fuel burns.   [2]

b Name the impurity present in some fuels that causes acid rain when the fuel burns.   [1]

c Why doesn't petrol produce sulfur dioxide when it is burnt?   [1]

[Total 4 marks]

9 The Earth's crust and top layer of the mantle are rigid and are broken into many tectonic plates.

a How fast do tectonic plates move?   [1]

b From which process does the energy come from that causes this movement?   [1]

c What two destructive events may occur at plate margins?   [2]

[Total 4 marks]

10 Many food additives are found in food that we buy.

a Give two reasons why additives may be added to our food.   [2]

b Chromatography can be used to see what particular colourings have been added to food. Describe how you would see if some of the green colouring found in some frozen peas contains the yellow colouring, tartrazine.   [4]

[Total 6 marks]

Physics P1a and P1b

1 Match the words **A**, **B**, **C** and **D** with the spaces **1–4** in the sentences below.

A light   **B** chemical
C uranium   **D** kinetic (movement)

In a nuclear power station, the fuel used is ___1___.

A wind turbine changes the ___2___ energy of the wind into electrical energy.

In a remote farm, a solar panel changes ___3___ energy into electrical energy.

The battery in a DVD remote changes ___4___ energy into electrical energy. [1]

2 The speed of electromagnetic waves is given by the equation:

speed = wavelength × frequency

a Which of the following waves is not an electromagnetic wave?

A gamma rays
B X-rays
C radio waves
D sound [1]

b The speed of all electromagnetic waves is 3.0×10^8 m/s. What is the frequency of microwaves of wavelength 0.02 m?

A 6.0×10^6 Hz
B 3.0×10^8 Hz
C 1.5×10^{10} Hz
D 6.7×10^{-11} Hz [1]

3 These questions are to do with the Universe.

a How do we know that the Universe is expanding?

A There are stars in the sky.
B The Earth's rotation gives us day and night.
C Our Solar System is expanding.
D All galaxies are moving away from each other. [1]

b What does 'red shift' mean?

A The light from a star moving away becomes longer in wavelength.
B The light from all stars becomes red.
C The light from a star moving towards us becomes shorter in wavelength.
D The Sun turns red during sunset. [1]

4 Smoke detectors use americium that emits alpha particles.

a What are alpha particles?

A electrons
B helium nuclei
C protons
D gamma rays [1]

b Which of the following statements is true about alpha particles?

A They are the least ionising radiation.
B They can only be stopped by lead of several metres thick.
C They can be deflected by a magnetic field.
D They travel at the speed of light. [1]

5 For a particular electric motor, 50 J of the electrical energy is transformed into 24 J of kinetic energy.

a Explain why the kinetic energy is not equal to the electrical energy. [1]

b Use the equation:

$$\text{efficiency} = \frac{\text{output useful energy}}{\text{total input energy}}$$

to calculate the efficiency of the motor. [3]

[Total 4 marks]

6 a Explain what is meant by the wavelength of a wave. [1]

b Light and microwaves are both electromagnetic waves. State two properties of electromagnetic waves. [2]

c Here are some possible statements about microwaves. Place a tick (✓) in the appropriate column. [3]

Statement	True	False
microwaves can be reflected by metal		
microwaves are the same as ultrasound		
microwaves can heat or burn body tissues		

d An insect on the surface of a pond, flaps its wings at a frequency of 200 Hz and creates ripples on the surface of the water of wavelength 0.01 m. Use the following equation to find the speed of the ripples on the surface of the water: speed = wavelength × frequency. [3]

[Total 9 marks]

7 Cobalt-60 has a half-life of about 5.0 years and it emits gamma rays.

a Describe one difference and one similarity between gamma rays and X-rays. [2]

b Explain what is meant by 'half-life' of an isotope. [1]

c Explain how gamma rays are used in the treatment of cancer. [2]

[Total 5 marks]

Additional Biology

1 Which part of an animal cell carries out each of the following functions?

a Controls the cell's activities. [1]

b Controls what enters and leaves the cell. [1]

c Where chemical reactions take place. [1]

[Total 3 marks]

2 a What is the function of a chloroplast in a plant cell? [1]

b List two other structures found in plant cells but not in animal cells. [2]

[Total 3 marks]

3 For the following food chain, sketch:

a a pyramid of numbers. [3]

b a pyramid of biomass. [3]

oak tree → caterpillars → great tits → fleas

[Total 6 marks]

4 a Explain why keeping hens in battery farms is cost effective. [3]

b Why are some people against battery farming? [1]

[Total 4 marks]

5 Explain how a person usually inherits Huntingdon's disease. [3]

6 a What is osmosis? [3]

b Describe what would happen to an animal cell if it were placed in distilled water. [2]

[Total 5 marks]

7 a Write down the word equation for photosynthesis. [2]

b Explain how leaves are adapted for photosynthesis. [4]

[Total 6 marks]

8 Use the food chain below to answer the following questions.

grass → antelope → lion

a What do the arrows in the food chain represent? [1]

b Why is the grass known as the producer? [1]

c Explain why only a small proportion of the sunlight energy available to the producer ends up as energy available to the antelope. [4]

[Total 6 marks]

9 Fur colour in mice is genetically determined. The dominant allele, B, causes brown fur, the recessive allele, b, causes black fur.

Construct a genetic diagram to explain how two brown mice can produce offspring with black fur. [3]

10 a Complete the table below to compare mitosis and meiosis. [4]

Mitosis	Meiosis

b Explain why gametes must be haploid. [2]

[Total 6 marks]

Additional Chemistry

1 Draw a diagram of an atom of helium which has two protons, two neutrons and two electrons. Add the following labels: neutron, electron, nucleus, proton. [5]

2 Explain why atoms are always neutral. [2]

3 Below is a diagram of a magnesium atom and a magnesium ion.

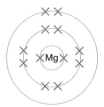 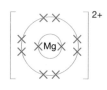

a An atom of oxygen is shown. Draw an oxygen ion. [2]

b When magnesium and oxygen react they form magnesium oxide. What type of bonding will there be in magnesium oxide? [1]

c Would you expect magnesium oxide to have a low or high boiling point? [1]

[Total 4 marks]

4 Use a data sheet for this question.
  a What is the relative formula mass of $CaCl_2$? [1]
  b Calculate the percentage by mass, of chlorine in $CaCl_2$. [2]

[Total 3 marks]

5 Explain why the rate of a reaction increases when the temperature is raised. [3]

Additional Physics

1 a On the axes below, draw a graph for an object:
  i travelling at a constant speed. [1]
  ii travelling with a constant acceleration. [1]

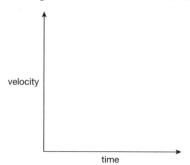

b What does the gradient of a velocity–time graph represent? [1]

c A racing car travelling at a speed of 40 m/s crashes into a safety barrier and comes to a halt after a time of 2.5 seconds. Calculate the average deceleration of the car. [3]

[Total 6 marks]

2 a For a particular journey, the distance travelled by a car in a time of 1 hour (3600 seconds) is 60 km. What is the average speed of the car in m/s? [3]

b A car travelling at 20 m/s has a braking distance of 20 m and a thinking distance of 10 m.
  i Explain what is meant by braking distance. [1]
  ii Determine the reaction time of the driver. [2]
  iii Calculate the stopping distance of the car at this speed. [1]
  iv State two factors that would increase the braking distance of the car. [2]

[Total 9 marks]

3 a Describe how the resistance of a light-dependent resistor (LDR) is affected by light. [1]

b i On the axes below, draw a graph to show the characteristic of a filament lamp. [2]

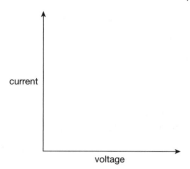

ii Explain how you can determine the resistance of the lamp at a particular voltage. [2]

iii Describe how the resistance of the lamp changes as the current in the lamp increases. [2]

[Total 7 marks]

4 A car of mass 800 kg is travelling on a level road at a constant velocity of 20 m/s.

a State and explain the value of the resultant force acting on the car. [2]

b Calculate the kinetic energy of the car in joules. [3]

c The driver applies the brakes for a period of 1.2 seconds. After this period of time, the velocity of the car decreases to 5 m/s. Calculate the deceleration of the car. [3]

[Total 8 marks]

5 **a** Define the term 'momentum'. [1]

b A 3000 kg truck is moving due North at a speed of 20 m/s.

i Calculate the momentum of the truck. [2]

ii What is the momentum of the truck when travelling at the same speed in a southerly direction?
Explain your answer. [2]

c The truck has a gentle collision with another truck. State two quantities conserved in the collision. [2]

[Total 7 marks]

6 The diagram below shows a circuit designed by a student to monitor the temperature in a room.

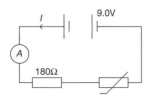

The total potential difference across the components is 9.0 V. The fixed resistor has resistance 180 Ω.

a At a particular temperature, the resistance of the thermistor is 120 Ω.

i Calculate the total resistance of the circuit. [2]

ii Calculate the current, I, from the battery. [2]

iii Calculate the total power dissipated in the circuit. [3]

b Explain how your answer to **aii** would change when the temperature of the thermistor is increased. [2]

[Total 9 marks]

7 **a** Explain what is meant by an isotope. [1]

b One of the isotopes of uranium is $^{235}_{92}$U.

i What is the atomic (proton) number for this isotope? [1]

ii Calculate the number of neutrons in the nucleus of this isotope. [2]

iii This isotope of uranium emits an alpha particle. State two properties of an alpha particle. [2]

c In a fission reaction, a neutron is absorbed by a nucleus of $^{235}_{92}$U. What is the nucleon (mass) number of the new isotope? [1]

[Total 7 marks]

8 A 20 kg box is lying on the floor.

a On the diagram above, draw an arrow to show the weight of the box. [1]

b The Earth's gravitational field on its surface is 9.8 N/kg. Calculate the weight of the box. [2]

c A person lifts the box through a vertical height of 1.2 m in a time of 0.5 seconds.

i Calculate the work done against gravity [3]

ii Calculate the power developed by the person. [3]

[Total 9 marks]

GCSE Biology

1 a Name the type of blood vessels that carry blood to respiring tissues. [1]

b Name the type of blood vessels that carry blood back to the heart. [1]

c Humans have a double circulation. Explain what this means. [2]

[Total 4 marks]

2 The following sentences describe stages in the production of beer.

A: Yeast is added to the solution.

B: Starch in barley grains is broken down into a sugary solution by enzymes.

C: Fermentation takes place to produce alcohol.

D: Hops are added to flavour the beer.

E: The sugary solution is extracted.

Put the letters for each stage in the correct order. One has been done for you.

Stage	1	2	3	4	5
Letter			A		

[4]

3 Complete the table about the different parts of blood.

Part of blood	Description
red blood cell	
	defends the body against disease
	liquid part of the blood
platelets	

[4]

4 a Explain how a healthy kidney produces urine. [3]

b Describe one advantage and one disadvantage of the use of kidney dialysis to treat patients with kidney failure. [2]

c What can doctors do to try and prevent a patient's body rejecting a kidney transplant? [2]

[Total 7 marks]

5 a Describe two changes that occur to the body during exercise. [2]

b Explain as fully as you can why these changes occur. [5]

[Total 7 marks]

GCSE Chemistry

1 Describe the reaction of sodium with water. [3]

2 a What do you understand by the term 'weak acid'? [1]

b Give an example of a weak acid. [1]

[Total 2 marks]

3 a Which two ions cause hardness in water? [2]

b What may be added to water in order to remove the hardness? [1]

c Describe another way of removing the hardness from water and explain how it works. [3]

d Give one disadvantage of hard water. [1]

e Give one reason why you might not want to remove the hardness from drinking water. [1]

[Total 8 marks]

4 a What are the two main food groups that provide us with energy in our diet. [2]

b What happens if you eat too much of these foods? [2]

c What problem can eating too many high energy foods lead to? [1]

d Draw an energy level diagram to show what happens when respiration occurs in your body. [4]

[Total 9 marks]

5 Some tests are carried out on some compounds. Identify the ion present from the results of the test.

Results of test	Ion present
gives a lilac flame test	
forms a rusty-brown precipitate when sodium hydroxide solution is added	
forms a blue precipitate when sodium hydroxide solution is added	
forms a white precipitate when first nitric acid, then silver nitrate is added	
forms a white precipitate when first hydrochloric acid, then barium chloride solution is added	
fizzes vigorously when dilute hydrochloric acid is added	

[6]

GCSE Physics

 A satellite is in a geostationary orbit above the equator.

  a Name the force that keeps the satellite in an orbit round the Earth. [1]

  b What is the period of a satellite in a geostationary orbit? [1]

  c The orbit of the satellite is a circle and it has a constant speed. Describe the force acting on the satellite and the acceleration of the satellite. [3]

  d What are satellites in a geostationary orbit used for? [1]

[Total 6 marks]

 a Describe the nature of the image produced in a plane mirror. [3]

  b Describe one difference between a diverging lens and a convex lens. [1]

  c The diagram below shows an object placed within the focal length of a convex lens.

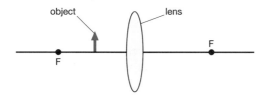

    i Construct a ray diagram to locate the position of the image produced by the lens. [3]

    ii Describe two properties of this image. [2]

[Total 9 marks]

Model answers

1. Which of the following describes the effect of oestrogen on the body?

   A Causes ovulation

   B Stimulates ovaries to produce FSH

   C Inhibits FSH production

   D Causes eggs to mature in the ovaries   [1]

   FSH stimulates the ovaries to produce oestrogen, which operates in a negative feedback mechanism to prevent the pituitary releasing any more FSH to prevent another egg maturing. So, the answer is C.

2. Which of the following health problems are linked to lack of food?

   A Obesity

   B Diabetes

   C Reduced resistance to infection

   D High blood pressure   [1]

   When a person does not get enough food they cannot fight diseases, because their white blood cells cannot destroy bacteria and viruses. This leads to reduced resistance to infection. So, the answer is C.

3. Which of the following statements about smoking is true?

   A Giving up smoking will not reduce the risk of dying from cancer.

   B Smoking relieves stress and so helps to lower blood pressure.

   C Passive smoking is harmless.

   D Pregnant women who smoke have smaller babies.   [1]

   Tobacco smoke contains carbon monoxide, which means the blood cannot carry as much oxygen as it should. The developing baby does not get enough oxygen and cannot grow properly, so the answer is D.

4. How many chromosomes are there in a human sperm cell?

   A 46

   B 26

   C 43

   D 23   [1]

A sperm cell contains just one copy of each chromosome. It fuses with an egg cell, which also contains one copy of each chromosome, to produce a zygote with pairs of each chromosome. The answer is D.

5. Which two of the following are most likely to be causes of extinction?

   A New diseases

   B An earthquake

   C New predators

   D A hurricane   [1]

   Whilst an earthquake and a hurricane may cause many deaths, there are still likely to be some survivors of each species to breed and maintain the population. New diseases and new predators may, over time, cause a species to become extinct as the balance between births and deaths changes. So, the answer is A and C.

6. Sometimes new forms of genes arise spontaneously. What is this called?

   A Fertilisation

   B Mutation

   C Cancer

   D Mitosis   [1]

   Changes in the base sequence of DNA may arise due to errors in 'copying' the DNA. These are called mutations (answer B).

7. Write down two possible health problems caused by malnutrition.   [2]

   Any two of the following would be accepted:
      Irregular periods in women.
      Reduced resistance to disease.
      Poor growth.
      Deficiency diseases, for example scurvy, rickets, night blindness.

8. Explain why oestrogen can be used in oral contraceptive pills.   [3]

   Oestrogen affects the pituitary gland, preventing it from releasing FSH. Without FSH, no eggs will mature inside the ovaries, so ovulation and pregnancy cannot occur.

9 Describe two advantages and two disadvantages of oral contraceptives. [4]

Any two advantages from: women can control when they want to have families, fewer unwanted pregnancies, easy to use.

Any two disadvantages from: no protection against sexually transmitted infections, expensive, increase in promiscuity

10 Below are some data collected to show the average number of different lichen species growing on tree barks at different distances from a city centre.

Distance from city centre (km)	Average number of lichen species in given area
8	0
12	5
16	10
20	25
24	40
32	40

a Describe the pattern shown by the data. [1]

The number of different lichen species increases as you get further away from the city centre.

b Where is air pollution the lowest? [1]

Furthest from the city centre (at 24/32 km from the city centre).

c Explain in as much detail as you can the relationship between the number of lichen species and the distance from the city centre. [2]

Lichens are sensitive to air pollution. The closer to the city centre, the more air pollution there is due to factories, traffic, etc. More lichen species grow where there is less air pollution further away from the city centre.

11 Explain how vaccinations against diseases such as measles prevent disease. [4]

Vaccines contain antigens, bacteria or viruses that do not harm us. When we are vaccinated, these stimulate white blood cells to produce antibodies against the antigens. On re-infection with the real disease, antibodies are produced more quickly than they would be otherwise, so the disease is cleared before symptoms appear.

Chemistry C1a and C1b

1 Match words A, B, C and D with the spaces in the sentences.

A magnesium carbonate B calcium oxide
C carbon dioxide D calcium carbonate

Limestone is a naturally occurring resource which contains the compound __1__. Limestone can be decomposed by heating it and it forms the gas __2__ and __3__ (quicklime). Carbonates of other metals such as __4__ decompose in the same way. [1]

Answers 1D 2C 3B 4A

2 Match the processes A, B, C and D with the reactions they bring about in 1, 2, 3 and 4.

A polymerisation   B thermal decomposition
C fractional distillation   D reduction

1 obtaining plastics from alkenes
2 obtaining iron from iron oxide
3 obtaining lime from limestone
4 obtaining petrol from crude oil [1]

Answers 1A 2D 3B 4C

In Q3–4 select the correct answer.

3 Plant oils are an important source of energy in our diet.
1 They are extracted from nuts, seeds and fish.
2 They are needed in our diet as they provide the materials for growth and repair.
3 They don't mix with water but they can be made into emulsions.
4 They can be hardened into spreadable fats by reacting with nickel at 60 °C. [1]

1 is incorrect, fish are not plants!

2 is incorrect, oils give energy and vitamins.

3 is correct.

4 is incorrect. Oils are reacted with hydrogen. Nickel is the catalyst.

4 Our atmosphere today has been much the same for the last 200 million years.
1 It contains about 80% oxygen.
2 It contains noble gases such as hydrogen and helium.
3 It contains 20% carbon dioxide and this percentage is increasing due to fossil fuel burning.
4 It contains about 20% oxygen almost none of which was present in the early atmosphere on Earth. [1]

1 is incorrect, nitrogen forms 80% of the air.

2 is incorrect, H_2 is not a noble gas.

3 is incorrect, only about 0.03% CO_2 is present.

4 is correct.

5 The symbol equation for the decomposition of calcium carbonate is: $CaCO_3 \rightarrow CaO + CO_2$

 a Explain how you know that this equation is balanced. [1]

There are the same number of each type of atom in the reactants and products.

 b What does the formula $CaCO_3$ tell you? [1]

$CaCO_3$ contains one atom of calcium and one atom of carbon for every three oxygen atoms.

 c Balance the equation below. [1]

 ___ Mg + ___ HCl → ___ $MgCl_2$ + ___ H_2

 Mg + 2HCl → $MgCl_2$ + H_2

3 **a** Describe the structure of a metal such as pure copper and use this to explain how copper may be easily bent. [2]

The metal atoms are arranged in layers which can slide over each other.

 b How does the addition of carbon to pure iron make the iron harder and stronger? [2]

Adding carbon atoms distorts the layers making it harder for them to slide over each other.

7 The diagram below shows methane.

```
        H
        |
   H — C — H
        |
        H
```

 a Draw a molecule of a saturated hydrocarbon with two carbons. [2]

```
      H   H
      |   |
  H — C — C — H
      |   |
      H   H
```

 b Draw a molecule of an unsaturated hydrocarbon with two carbons. [2]

```
  H             H
    \          /
     C  =  C
    /          \
  H             H
```

8 Noble gases are very unreactive but they still have many uses. Give examples of two different noble gases and state a use for each.

Gas 1 Neon   Use for gas 1: In discharge lamps [2]

Gas 2 Helium   Use for gas 2: In balloons [2]

Physics P1a and P1b

1 Which of the following quantities is not a scalar?

A speed

B distance

C velocity

D time [1]

A scalar quantity has only magnitude; whereas a vector quantity has both magnitude and direction. In the list above, all quantities are scalar apart from velocity. Velocity is a vector quantity. Hence the answer is C.

2 Two cars X and Y are travelling on a road at the same constant speed. Car X has a greater mass than car Y. Which statement below is incorrect?

A Both cars have the same weight.

B Car X has greater momentum than car Y.

C Both cars have the same momentum.

D Both cars are accelerating. [1]

The weight of a car depends on its mass and acceleration due to gravity (weight = mg). Since the cars have different masses, they cannot have the same weight. Hence A is incorrect. Momentum is defined as:

momentum = mass × velocity.

Since car X has a greater mass but the same speed, its momentum is definitely more than that of car Y. B is the correct answer.

C is incorrect because the cars do have different masses and D is also incorrect because the acceleration of each car is zero.

3 An electric heater of rating 2800 W is used to warm a small room in a house.

a What is the power of the heater in kilowatts? [1]

1 kW is equal to 1000 watts, therefore the power of the heater is 2.8 kW.

b Explain what is meant by the kilowatt hour. [2]

The kilowatt hour is the energy transformed when an appliance of power 1 kW is operated for a time of 1 hour.

c Calculate the cost of using this heater for a period of 24 hours given that the cost of each kWh is 14p. [5]

Number of kWh = power (kW) × time (hours)

Number of kWh = 2.8 × 24

Number of kWh = 67.2

Cost = number of kWh × cost per kWh

Cost = 67.2 × 14p

Cost = 940.8 p ≈ £9.41

4 Radio telescopes are used to image distant galaxies using microwaves.

a Write two things you know about microwaves. [2]

Microwaves are electromagnetic waves.

Microwaves travel through a vacuum at the speed of light (300 000 000 m/s).

b The microwave spectrum from all galaxies being observed show a red shift.

i What does 'red shift' mean? [1]

The entire spectrum from a galaxy is shifted to longer wavelengths.

ii What does red shift tell us about the Universe? [2]

Red shift implies that all galaxies are moving away from each other, and therefore the Universe is expanding.

Additional Biology

1 Sue and Mick are expecting a baby. Neither suffers from cystic fibrosis. However, there is a 1 in 4 chance that their baby will inherit cystic fibrosis. Explain why – you may use a genetic diagram to help you. [4]

Cystic fibrosis is caused by a recessive allele. In order for a child to inherit the disease, both parents must be carriers. A carrier does not suffer from the disease. The genetic diagram below shows that the cc genotype for cystic fibrosis occurs with a 1 in 4 chance.

	C	c
C	CC	Cc
c	Cc	cc — has CF

2 **a** Explain why biological washing powders may contain protease and lipases. [1]

Proteases and lipases will digest food stains.

b Why will biological washing powders not work properly at high temperatures? [2]

The enzymes will be denatured at high temperatures, so the stains will no longer be removed.

3 Describe the function of the liver in the digestive system. [4]

The liver produces bile, which enters the small intestine along with the stomach contents. Bile is alkaline and neutralises the acidic contents from the stomach, providing the optimum pH for enzyme function in the small intestine. Bile also emulsifies fats, breaking them down into smaller droplets to increase the surface area for enzyme action.

4 Describe and explain as fully as you can the changes that occur in the skin when body temperature is too high. [4]

Blood capillaries close to the surface of the skin dilate, so more blood flows to the surface and more heat is lost. Sweat glands release sweat, which cools the body as it evaporates.

5 **a** State two waste products that must be removed from the body. [2]

Any two will be accepted from: urea, carbon dioxide, excess water, excess ions.

b Why must the body remove waste products? [1]

Otherwise they would build up and become toxic (poison the body).

Additional Chemistry

1 Elements are often shown in the periodic table.

a In what order are the elements shown in the periodic table? [1]

In order of atomic (or proton) number.

b What can you say about the number of electrons in the outer shell of an element in group 2? [1]

It will have two electrons in the outer shell.

c Draw a diagram to show the electron arrangement of an atom of calcium. [2]

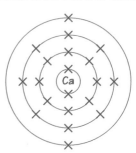

2 Calcium carbonate decomposes according to the equation: $CaCO_3 \rightarrow CaO + CO_2$.

a What is the relative formula mass of calcium carbonate? [1]

$40 + 12 + (3 \times 16) = 100$

b What is the relative formula mass of calcium oxide? [1]

$40 + 16 = 56$

c If you fully decomposed 50 g of calcium carbonate, what mass of calcium oxide would you expect to produce? [1]

100 g of $CaCO_3$ gives 56 g of CaO so 50 g will give 28 g of CaO

3 Some marble chips ($CaCO_3$) are placed in a flask with some dilute hydrochloric acid and they react forming carbon dioxide gas.

a Give three ways of speeding this reaction up. [3]

Heat the acid, powder the $CaCO_3$ and increase the concentration of the acid.

b Give two ways of measuring the rate of this reaction. [2]

Measure how quickly the flask loses mass.

Measure how quickly the gas is made by collecting it in a gas syringe.

4 Electrolysis of sodium chloride is carried out using the apparatus below.

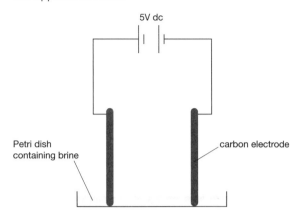

5V dc

Petri dish containing brine

carbon electrode

a What gas forms at the positive electrode? [1]

Chlorine (*because it has negative ions*).

b What gas forms at the negative electrode? [1]

Hydrogen (*because it has positive ions*).

c What solution forms in the petri dish? [1]

Sodium hydroxide solution

Additional Physics

1 A shopper in a supermarket gently places a 6.0 kg bag of potatoes on a conveyor belt moving at a speed of 0.25 m/s. A fault causes the conveyor belt to stop over a period of 0.50 seconds.

a Calculate the momentum of the bag of potatoes when it was travelling at a speed of 0.25 m/s. [3]

momentum = mass × velocity
momentum = 6.0 × 0.25
momentum = 1.5 kg m/s

b What is the resultant force acting on the bag when it was moving at a constant speed? [1]

The resultant force must be zero because the bag is not accelerating.

c What is the final momentum of the bag? [1]

The final momentum is zero because the bag is not moving.

d Determine the size of the force that stops the bag. [3]

$$force = \frac{change\ in\ momentum}{time}$$

$$force = \frac{(0 - 1.5)}{0.50}$$

force = − 3.0 N (The minus sign means the bag has a deceleration.)

2 A student connects up the following circuit.

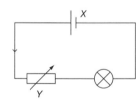

a Name the component X. [1]

The component X is a cell.

b Name the component Y. [1]

The component Y is a variable resistor.

c The potential difference across the lamp is 6.0 V when the current in the circuit is 0.2 A.

i Calculate the resistance of the lamp. [3]

$$resistance = \frac{potential\ difference}{current}$$

$$resistance = \frac{6.0}{0.2}$$

resistance = 30 Ω

ii Calculate the power of the lamp. [3]

power = potential difference × current
power = 6.0 × 0.2
power = 1.2 W

GCSE Biology

1 a What is anaerobic respiration? [1]

Respiration in the absence of oxygen.

b When might anaerobic respiration occur? [1]

After vigorous exercise or long periods of exercise.

c Name the waste product of anaerobic respiration in humans. [1]

Lactic acid

d Explain what is meant by the term 'oxygen debt'. [3]

Lactic acid builds up in muscles during periods of anaerobic respiration. After exercise has stopped, the breathing rate must remain higher than usual to take in extra oxygen to oxidise the lactic acid.

2 a What is the function of a red blood cell? [1]

To transport oxygen around the body.

b Explain how a red blood cell carries out this function. [4]

Red blood cells contain the pigment haemoglobin. Haemoglobin binds reversibly with oxygen to form oxyhaemoglobin. Haemoglobin binds oxygen at the lungs and releases it at respiring tissues.

3 Explain, as fully as you can, why the alveoli are an excellent surface for gas exchange. [4]

The alveoli have a large surface area for diffusion to occur. The moist surface aids diffusion. They have very thin walls to minimise the distance for diffusion of oxygen and carbon dioxide. Each alveolus is surrounded by a rich network of blood capillaries for the exchange of gases.

4 a What is active transport? [2]

The transport of substances against a concentration gradient, which requires energy from respiration.

b Explain why root hair cells must absorb mineral ions from the soil by active transport. [3]

The mineral ions are in a very low concentration in soil. There is a higher concentration of minerals inside the plant cells, so the mineral ions must be absorbed against the concentration gradient using active transport.

5 Describe three features usually found in industrial fermenters. [6]

Any three from the following list. One mark is allocated for each feature and one for each description.

An air supply is needed to provide oxygen for the microorganisms' respiration.

A stirrer is needed to keep the microorganisms in suspension and maintain an even temperature.

A water-cooled jacket removes the heat produced by the respiring microorganisms.

A pH sensor is required to check that the pH is kept to the optimum level for microorganisms' growth.

A temperature sensor is used to check temperature is kept to optimum level.

GCSE Chemistry

1 Complete this table to show the properties of chlorine. [4]

Name	Formula	State at room temperature	Colour	Charge on ions
chlorine	Cl_2	gas	pale green	1-

2 Refer to the diagram below and answer the following questions.

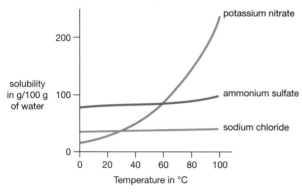

a Which solid is most soluble at 20 °C? [1]

ammonium sulfate

b Which solid is most soluble at 100 °C [1]

potassium nitrate

c If the same volume of each solution was cooled from 80 °C to 40 °C, which would make the greatest mass of crystals? [1]

potassium nitrate

3 Exothermic reactions give out heat energy. Using ideas about bond making and breaking, explain why the reaction between methane and oxygen is exothermic. [3]

More energy is given out when bonds are formed in the products than is taken in when the bonds in the reactants are broken.

4 Modern instrumental methods are now employed in many analytical laboratories.

a Give two advantages of these instruments. [2]

They are accurate, sensitive and rapid and are particularly useful when small amounts of sample are available. (Any two of these.)

b Name a method particularly suited to identifying the presence of a particular element and give one industry where this is used. [2]

Atomic absorption spectroscopy which is used in the iron industry.

GCSE Physics

1 The night sky is full of stars and distant galaxies.

a Explain what is meant by a galaxy. [1]

A galaxy has millions of stars held together by the attractive force of gravity.

b Describe how a star is formed from interstellar dust and hydrogen gas. [4]

Gravitational attraction causes the dust and gas particles to collapse.

As they do so, the kinetic energy of the particles increases and this causes the temperature to increase.

Eventually, fusion reactions occur between the hydrogen nuclei.

This releases energy and a star is born.

c Describe the fate of a star having a mass similar to that of our Sun. [4]

At the end of its life, the star starts to expand.

As it expands it becomes cooler and becomes a red giant.

Eventually, the outer layers of the red giant are blown away as a planetary nebula.

The core left behind is a white dwarf.

NOW TRY THIS ANSWERS

IN CONTROL – pages 6 and 7
a Chemical, secreted, glands, bloodstream, target, slower, longer, water, sugar
b Oestrogen, oestrogen, FSH, LH, oestrogen
c False, true, false, false, false, true, false

KEEPING HEALTHY – pages 8 and 9
a False, true, false, false, false
b Human cells, cells, pathogens, about 1000
c i Pathogens ii antibody iii antibiotic iv lymphocytes v phagocytes
d Ingest, digest/destroy, antibodies, antigens, quickly, symptoms

REPRODUCTION AND GENES – pages 10 and 11
a Asexual, identical, parent, sexual, gametes, fertilisation, offspring, variation
b i Fertilisation ii Gamete iii DNA iv Nucleus v Chromosomes
c ii, v, iv, i, iii
d False, true, false, true, true, false

EVOLUTION AND EXTINCTION – pages 12 and 13
a Features, behaviours, suited/adapted, environment, survive, reproduce
b True, true, false, false, false, true
c ii, iv, iii, i, v
d i, iii, iv

OUR IMPACT ON THE ENVIRONMENT – pages 14 and 15
a Increasing, longer, farming, health, disease, building, agriculture, waste
b Air, water, water, air, air, land, land
c Greenhouse, heat, re-radiated, hotter, greenhouse, global warming, fossil fuels, deforestation
d Non-renewable, renewable, non-renewable, renewable, renewable, renewable, renewable

ALL ABOUT ATOMS – pages 16 and 17
a i Atom ii Symbol iii Group iv Elements v Nucleus vi Electrons
b Co
c NO
d Balanced equations show that atoms are not lost or gained in chemical reactions
e $+$, $\rightarrow$, one, one, oxygen
f i T ii F – it has many uses iii F – glass is made using limestone iv F – quicklime is calcium oxide

METALS FROM ORES – pages 18 and 19
a i Gold ii Iron iii Carbon iv Iron oxide v Ore
b 96, brittle, soft, alloy, stronger, corrode rust
c i Titanium ii bend iii bridges
d i T ii F – doesn't corrode iii F – too soft, not too hard iv T v F – there is lots of aluminium ore

CRUDE OIL – pages 20 and 21
a Mixture, compounds, fractional distillation, boiling point

b i Compounds ii C_nH_{2n+2} iii saturated iv C_7H_{14}
c 3, 5, 2, 1, 4
d CO_2 and H_2O, SO_2, SO_2, S, H_2O, CO_2, solid particles

CRACKING AND POLYMERS – pages 22 and 23
a i Small hydrocarbons ii C_nH_{2n} iii C_7H_{14} iv Saturated
v
$$\begin{array}{c}
H \quad\quad H \\
| \quad\quad\quad | \\
C=C-C-H \\
| \quad\quad\quad | \\
H \quad\quad H
\end{array}$$
vi Small molecules
b Steam, catalyst, ethene, steam, plastics, poly(ethene), alkanes, fuels
c i Poly(ethene) ii Poly(propene) iii Poly(styrene) iv Poly(butene)
d i F – it is difficult to separate them ii T iii F – many make toxic fumes when burnt iv T

FOOD CHEMISTRY – pages 24 and 25
a Energy, nutrients, mustard, emulsion, coat, texture
b Unsaturated: C_3H_6, decolourises bromine, contains at least one C=C double bond, general formula is C_nH_{2n}
Saturated: methane, iodine solution stays brown C_3H_8, contains only C-C single bonds
c i ACD ii BEF iii AD iv C

THE EARTH AND ITS ATMOSPHERE – pages 26 and 27
a i Large piece of Earth's crust and upper mantle ii Provides energy for convection currents in the mantle iii A few metres every century iv Occur at plate boundaries v Has occurred since its formation
b i Nitrogen ii Oxygen iii Water vapour iv Carbon dioxide v Water vapour
c i Neon ii Neon or argon iii Helium
d DOWN, DOWN, UP, UP, DOWN, DOWN, DOWN, DOWN, UP

THERMAL ENERGY – pages 28 and 29
a i, ii, iv
b i, ii
c i insulator ii Poor iii Close together

EFFICIENT USE OF ENERGY – pages 30 and 31
a Kinetic, chemical, heat
b i Remains stationary ii Watts iii Joules iv Second
c i, ii

ELECTRICITY – pages 32 and 33
a Electrical, light, hot, portable
b i, ii, iv
c

V	C						L
O	A					A	
L	B				N		
T	L		L	O	S	S	D
A	E		I			I	
G	T					R	
E	A					G	
N	T	N	E	R	R	U	C

GENERATING ELECTRICITY – pages 34 and 35
a Coil, magnet, voltmeter, wires
b Renewable: straw, manure
Non-renewable: coal, uranium, crude oil
c Electricity, uranium, water, steam
d i, iii

ELECTROMAGNETIC WAVES – pages 36 and 37
a m/s, m, Hz
b iii, iv
c Ultraviolet waves, X-rays, gamma rays
d Radio waves, microwaves, infrared waves, visible light

RADIOACTIVITY – pages 38 and 39
a ii, iii
b Tracer, pass, increase
c

		B				
R	E			M		
E	T		U			
C	A	T				
N		A	L	P	H	A
A	T					
C	E	L	L	S		
	G	A	M	M	A	

THE UNIVERSE – pages 40 and 41
a i, iv
b Moon, Mars, Sun, Pluto
c 2, 1, 3, 4
d Red shift, space is at −270 °C, galaxies are moving away from us

CELL ACTIVITY – pages 42 and 43
a i Cytoplasm ii Chloroplasts iii Mitochondria iv Nucleus v Ribosomes vi Cell membrane
b False, false, true, false, true
c Diffusion, osmosis, diffusion, diffusion, osmosis, diffusion
d Speed, protein, folded, one, denatured, temperature, pH, used

PLANT NUTRITION – pages 44 and 45
a v, iii, vi, i, ii, iv
b ii, iii, ii, i, iii, ii, i
c Temperature, carbon dioxide, light, carbon dioxide
d Minerals, solution, roots, proteins, magnesium, chlorophyll, deficiency, poor, yellow

ENERGY AND MATTER – pages 46 and 47
a i Herbivore ii Carnivore iii Producer iv Omnivore
b Producer, energy, biomass, carnivore
c Lost, waste, movement, heat, limiting, temperature, heat, movement
d True, false, false, true, false, true

FOOD AND ENERGY – pages 48 and 49
a i Gall bladder ii Large intestine iii Oesophagus iv Liver v Stomach
b Stomach, stomach, small intestine, liver, pancreas, stomach
c Aerobic, energy, food, oxygen, breathing, mitochondria, carbon dioxide, exhaling, muscle, body temperature
d False, false, true, false, true, true, false

HOMEOSTASIS – pages 50 and 51

a Lungs = ii; Kidneys = iii, iv, vi, vii; Pancreas = ii; Skin = v; Liver = i

b Too cold, too cold, too hot, too hot, too hot, too cold

c Water, ions, concentrated, water, osmosis, shrink, dilute, enter, osmosis, swell, burst

d **i** Glycogen **ii** Glucagon **iii** Pancreas **iv** Hormone **v** Glucose **vi** Insulin **vii** Liver

INHERITANCE – pages 52 and 53

a ii, v, iii, iv, i, vi

b Mitosis, mitosis, meiosis, meiosis, mitosis, meiosis

c **i** Alleles **ii** Homozygous **iii** Dominant **iv** Heterozygous **v** Gene

d Faulty, inherited, cystic fibrosis, recessive, carriers, four, dominant, two

LOOKING MORE CLOSELY AT THE ATOM – pages 54 and 55

a **i** Electrons **ii** –1 **iii** Nucleus **iv** Protons, **v** protons + neutrons

b 20, 20, 20, (2,8,8,2)

c Compound, ion, positive, neon, negative, noble, lattice

d 1, 1+, krypton, 7, 1–, krypton

STRUCTURE AND BONDING – pages 56 and 57

a **i** Ions **ii** Electrostatic **iii** High **iv** Molten, **v** Weak

b Sharing, simple, strong, weak, low, do not, neutral

c

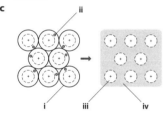

MASS AND MOLES – pages 58 and 59

a **i** 35.5 **ii** 20 **iii** 6 **iv** 8 **v** 12

b 44, 74, 18, 27, 88, 35

c 23 g, 46 g, 2 g, 2, 80 g, 0.2 g

d Yields, completion, product, lost, economic

RATES OF REACTION – pages 60 and 61

a Increase, decrease, increase, increase

b **i** More frequent collisions and more energetic collisions **ii** More frequent collisions **iii** More frequent collisions **iv** More frequent collisions

c Faster, costs, catalysts, transition metals

d Exothermic, endothermic, exothermic, endothermic, exothermic, endothermic, exothermic

EQUILIBRIUM REACTIONS – pages 62 and 63

a Haber, Reactants, Ammonia, Reversible, Temperature

b **i** Nitrogen and hydrogen **ii** Ammonia **iii** Iron **iv** 450 °C **v** 200 atm

c Increase, increase, increase, increase, increase

d Increase, increase, increase, decrease, increase, no effect, decrease, increase

IONS IN SOLUTION – pages 64 and 65

a

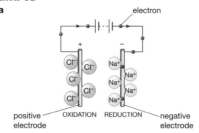

b Reduction, reduction, oxidation, oxidation, reduction

c Calcium carbonate, magnesium chloride, sodium sulfate, copper nitrate, lead sulfate

d Alkali, nitric, indicator, hydroxide, hydrogen, water

THE WAY THINGS MOVE – pages 66 and 67

a **i** m/s **ii** 10 km **iii** yes

b ii, iii

c

		D	E	E	P	S
T	N	E	I	D	A	R	G
		T				
		I				
		M				
V	E	L	O	C	I	T	Y
D	I	S	T	A	N	C	E

SPEED UP OR SLOW DOWN – pages 68 and 69

a ii, iii,

b i, ii, iv

c 6 m, braking, thinking, stopping

ENERGY, WORK AND MOMENTUM – pages 70 and 71

a **i** Remains stationary **ii** Energy **iii** Joules (J) **iv** Newtons (N)

b **i** Kinetic **ii** Elastic strain energy **iii** Heat

c ii, iii and iv

d Seatbelts, airbags, crumple zone

STATIC ELECTRICITY – pages 72 and 73

a ii, iv

b Spark, air, dangerous, fumes

c

	T	H	G	I	L		
		E				P	
	A	D	R	U	M	O	
		T				W	
		I				D	
	N	I	M	A	G	E	
		G				R	

CURRENTS IN CIRCUITS – pages 74 and 75

a Complete, less, dim

b i, iii

c Filament lamp, thermistor

d ↑, ↓, ↑, ↓,

MAINS ELECTRICITY AND POWER – pages 76 and 77

a ii, iii, iv

b Earth connection is loose; neutral and live wires need to be swapped; grip needs to be secured

c **i** Coulomb **ii** Ampere **iii** Volt **iv** Joule **v** Watt

NUCLEAR PHYSICS – pages 78 and 79

a Electron, ion, proton, alpha particle

b 235, 90, 231

c ii, iii, iv

EXCHANGE – pages 80 and 81

a Osmosis, diffusion, active transport, diffusion/osmosis, active transport, active transport

b Exchange, surface area, diffusion, active transport, intestine, villi, large, diffusion

c Roots, leaves, roots, diffusion, active transport, osmosis

d Stomata = ii, v, viii; leaves = iii, vi; roots = i, iv, vii

BREATHING – pages 82 and 83

a **i** Alveoli **ii** Ribcage **iii** Diaphragm **iv** Rib muscles **v** Bronchi **vi** Bronchioles

b Contract, raised, increases, greater, flattened, in

c Oxygen, diffuses, capillaries, blood, oxygenated, carbon dioxide, exhale

d

R	I		O		D			
I	N		X		I		T	
B	H		Y	B	F		R	
C	A		G	R	F		A	
A	L	V	E	O	L	U	S	C
G	E		N	N	U	S		H
E			C	N	I			A
			H	G	O			A
				I	N			

CIRCULATION – pages 84 and 85

a v, iii, i, vi, iv, ii

b **i** Atrium **ii** Heart **iii** Left **iv** Red **v** Blue **vi** Valves

c Veins, arteries, arteries, capillaries, arteries, veins/capillaries, veins, veins, veins, arteries

d Oxygen, fighting disease, platelets, haemoglobin, carbon dioxide, plasma

EXERCISE AND RESPIRATION – pages 86 and 87

a Respiration, oxygen, carbon dioxide, breathing, exhaling

b Aerobic, anaerobic, aerobic, anaerobic, aerobic, anaerobic, aerobic, anaerobic

c Oxygen, anaerobic respiration, incomplete, small, energy, quick, lactic, oxygen, breathing, heart, oxidise, carbon dioxide, water

d True, false, true, false, true, true, false

THE KIDNEYS – pages 88 and 89

a **i** Kidneys **ii** Excretion **iii** Ureter **iv** Urea **v** Urethra

b Suppresses, less, less, large, dilute

c Urea, glucose, week, vein, diffusion

MICROBIOLOGY – pages 90 and 91

a Yeast, oxygen, anaerobically, fermentation, carbon dioxide, alcohol, brewing, wine, rise

b **i** Yeast **ii** carbon dioxide **iii** aerobic **iv** bacteria **v** anaerobic **vi** ethanol

c **i** Outlet tap **ii** pH probe **iii** Temperature probe **iv** Nutrient medium **v** Water-cooled jacket **vi** Air supply

d

[crossword grid with letters: I, S / F N B, T / E O A, E / R C A G A R, R / M T U L, I / E E R A, L / N R I, I / T, T S / Y E A S T, E]

PERIODIC TABLE – pages 92 and 93

a 5, 2, 3, 4, 1, 6, 7
b i, iii, v, vi
c i, iv, v, vi, vii, viii
d i, iv, v, vi, vii

ACIDS AND ALKALIS – pages 94 and 95

a 3, 2, 5, 1, 4
b i, ii, iv, v
c i 18.00 ii 0.036 iii 0.036 iv 1.44

WATER – pages 96 and 97

a 6, 1, 3, 4, 2, 5
b $(NH_4)_2SO_4$, NaCl, KNO_3, KNO_3
c Hard, hard, hard, soft, soft
d i Solids ii Dissolved solids iii Dissolved solids iv Microorganisms

ENERGY CHANGES IN CHEMICAL REACTIONS – pages 98 and 99

a 2, 7, 1, 6, 5, 3, 4
b Energy, calories, carbohydrates (or fats), fats (or carbohydrates), obese
c 2640 kJ, 3338 kJ, 698 kJ, exothermic

CHEMICAL ANALYSIS – pages 100 and 101

a Cu^{2+}, Li^+, Al^{3+}, Na^+, Fe^{3+}
b i Bromide ion ii Sulfate ion iii Iodide ions iv Carbonate ion
c Organic, colourless, unsaturated, double
d ii = B iii = C iv = A, B C and D
v = A, B, C and D vi = A

TURNING AND CIRCLES – pages 102 and 103

a Force, will not, centre
b ii, iii
c Gravitational, attractive, planets, small

LIGHT AND SOUND – pages 104 and 105

a

[crossword grid with letters: H / P V E, E / I A, R / T R C N O T E / C U Z / H U / M / S S E N D U O L]

b i Hertz ii Longitudinal iii Kidney

MOTORS, GENERATORS AND STARS – pages 106 and 107

a Battery, wire frame, magnet
b Strength of magnetic field, speed of rotation, number of turns
c Wire, iron ring, alternating current supply
d Blackhole, Dwarf, Elements, Galaxy, Hydrogen or Hole, Star or Supernova, Universe

ANSWERS TO EXAM–STYLE QUESTIONS

Biology B1a and B1b

1 1A, 2D, 3B, 4C
2 1C, 2A, 3B, 4D
3 1D, 2C, 3B, 4A,
4 B
5 1C, 2A, 3B, 4D
6 1C, 2A, 3B, 4D
7 a Two from: nicotine, tar, carbon monoxide, particulates/smoke
  b One from: nicotine – addictive, tar – causes cancer, carbon monoxide – reduces amount of oxygen carried in blood, particulates/smoke – coughing/damage to cilia
8 Slows reaction time, impairs judgement, blurred vision, slower to respond to hazards, increased sense of confidence
9 Trees not photosynthesising, less carbon dioxide taken in, burning/decomposition of trees releases carbon dioxide, increased carbon dioxide causes increased greenhouse effect/global warming
10 Unsightly/visual pollution, air pollution from increased traffic due to transportation of limestone, noise pollution from traffic, noise pollution from quarry, e.g. explosives used
11 Two from: new predators, new diseases, new competitors, environmental change

Chemistry C1a and C1b

1 1B, 2C, 3D, 4A
2 1B, 2D, 3A, 4C
3 A
4 B
5 B
6 a An ore is a rock that contains enough metal to make it economic to extract it
  b Advantage: it provides employment Disadvantages: it may be noisy/can create a lot of extra road traffic/may create a lot of dust
7 a Make it brittle
  b An alloy is a mixture of metals (or a metal and carbon in the case of steel)
  c High carbon steel is very strong
8 a Carbon dioxide and water vapour
  b Sulfur
  c The sulfur is removed before the petrol is burnt
9 a Very slowly, a few centimetres a year
  b Radioactive decay
  c Earthquakes and volcanoes
10 a Any two from: to preserve/improve flavour/improve appearance
  b Crush the peas and extract the green colouring using a solvent; draw a line across the base of a strip of filter paper and add a spot of the green solution and a spot of tartrazine onto the line; place the filter paper into some solvent in a beaker; allow the solvent to creep up the filter paper and see if there is a spot at the same level as the tartrazine

Physics P1a and P1b

1 1C, 2D, 3A, 4B
2 a D
  b C
3 a D
  b A
4 a B
  b C
5 a Some of the energy is lost as heat due to friction
  b 48 %
6 a The wavelength is the distance between two neighbouring peaks
  b Transverse waves and can travel through a vacuum
  c

Statement	True	False
microwaves can be reflected by metal	✓	
microwaves are the same as ultrasound		✓
microwaves can heat or burn body tissues	✓	

  d 2.0 m/s
7 a Difference: gamma rays have a shorter wavelength (or higher frequency) than X-rays; Similarity: both are transverse waves
  b The half-life of an isotope is the average time for half of the nuclei to decay
  c Several gamma ray sources are pointed towards the cancerous cells in the patient; the energy of the gamma rays destroys the cancerous cells

Additional Biology

1 a Nucleus
  b Cell membrane
  c Cytoplasm
2 a Where photosynthesis takes place
  b Cell wall, permanent vacuole
3 a

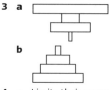

  b

4 a Limits their movement, temperature is controlled, less energy lost through movement and heat
  b Cruel/unnecessary, people could just pay more for free range produce
5 Caused by a dominant allele; one parent will be a sufferer; only one dominant allele must be inherited
6 a Diffusion of water molecules; from a dilute to a more concentrated solution; across a partially permeable membrane
  b Water would enter the cell by osmosis; the cell would swell/burst
7 a carbon dioxide + water $\rightarrow$ glucose + oxygen
The second mark is for putting sunlight above the arrow
  b Tiny pores (stomata) allow carbon dioxide to diffuse into the leaf; large surface area to capture sunlight; veins to carry water and minerals from the roots; thin so sunlight and carbon dioxide can reach photosynthesising cells
8 a Flow of energy
  b It makes its own food, rather than eating

c Some light does not fall on the leaves, some light passes through the leaves, some light is reflected back off the leaves, some light is the wrong wavelength, some is used for respiration in the plant, not all parts of the plant are eaten by the antelope

9

	B	b
B	BB	Bb
b	Bb	(bb)

10 a

Mitosis	Meiosis
2 daughter cells produced	4 daughter cells produced
occurs in somatic/ body cells	occurs to form gametes
(2 sets of chromosomes) daughter cells are diploid	daughter cells are haploid (1 set of chromosomes)
cells divide once	cells divide twice

b The number of chromosomes must first be halved because gametes fuse at fertilisation - each brings one set of chromosomes - to keep the chromosome number the same, otherwise it would keep increasing

Additional Chemistry

1

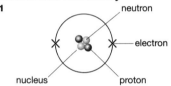

neutron
electron
nucleus
proton

2 Atoms are neutral because they have the same number of protons (with 1+ charge) as they have electrons (with 1– charge)

3 a

$2-$

b Ionic
c High melting point
4 Relative formula mass of $CaCl_2$ is 111
b Percentage chlorine = $\frac{71}{111}$ = 64 %

5 As the temperature is raised the particles gain more kinetic energy and move around faster; they collide more frequently and with more energy; successful collisions therefore occur more frequently

Additional Physics
1 a i and **ii**

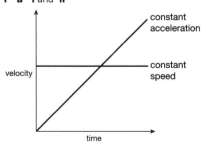

constant acceleration
constant speed
velocity
time

b The gradient is equal to acceleration
c Acceleration = -16 m/s^2 or deceleration = 16 m/s^2

2 a Average speed = 16.7 m/s
b i The braking distance is the distance travelled by the car from the moment the brakes are applied until the car stops
ii Reaction time = 0.5 s
iii Stopping distance = 30 m
iv The braking distance will increase if the speed is greater or the road is slippery (for example, ice)
3 a The resistance of the LDR decreases as the intensity of light falling on it increases
b i

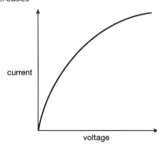

current
voltage

ii Read off the current for that particular voltage from the graph; use the equation:
resistance = $\frac{\text{voltage}}{\text{current}}$
to calculate the resistance
iii The resistance of the lamp increases as the filament gets hotter and the electrons collide more frequently with the vibrating atoms
4 a The resultant force is zero because there is no acceleration
b kinetic energy = $\frac{1}{2}mv^2 = \frac{1}{2} \times 800 \times 20^2$ = 160 000 J
c acceleration = change in velocity × time
$a = \frac{5 - 20}{1.2}$ = -12.5 m/s^2
(The minus sign means deceleration.)
5 a momentum = mass × velocity
b i momentum = 3000 × 20 = 60 000 kg m/s
ii momentum is a vector quantity, so the momentum will be $-60\,000$ kg m/s
c Momentum and total energy will be conserved
6 a i total resistance = 120 + 180 = 300 Ω
ii $I = \frac{V}{R} = \frac{9.0}{300}$ = 0.03A
iii $P = VI = 9.0 \times 0.03 = 0.27$ W
b The resistance of the thermistor will decrease; this decreases the total resistance of the circuit so the current I will decrease.
7 a A nucleus of an element with the same number of protons but a different number of neutrons
b i 92
ii Number of neutrons = 235 – 92 = 143
iii Has a positive charge; has two protons and two neutrons
c 236
8 a

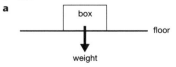

box
floor
weight

b weight = mg = 20 × 9.8 = 196 N
c i work done = force × distance moved in the direction of the force
work done = 196 × 1.2 = 235.2 J ≈ 240 J
ii power = work done × time
power = $\frac{235.2}{0.5}$ ≈ 470 W

GCSE Biology

1 a Arteries
b Veins
c One circulation goes to the lungs, the other to the body

2 1B, 2E, 3A, 4C, 5D

3 Red blood cell – carries oxygen around the body; white blood cell – defends the body against disease; plasma – liquid part of the blood; platelets – involved in clotting

4 a Filters the blood; reabsorbs sugar, some ions and some water; releases excess ions, excess water and all urea
b One advantage from: widely available to everyone, no problem with supply, no issue with rejection;
One disadvantage from: inconvenient and time-consuming, patient must be connected for many hours to a machine
c Use a donor kidney of a similar 'tissue-type' to the patient; use drugs to suppress the immune system

5 a Heart rate increases, breathing rate/depth increases
b More energy required during exercise; tissues respire more quickly so more oxygen is required; breathing rate/depth increases to obtain more oxygen and more carbon dioxide needs to be exhaled; glucose, oxygen and carbon dioxide are carried in the blood; the heart must beat faster to transport blood to the cells more quickly

GCSE Chemistry

1 Sodium reacts vigorously with water making hydrogen gas and an alkaline solution of sodium hydroxide

2 a A weak acid is only partly split up into its ions
b One from: ethanoic, citric, lactic, carbonic

3 a Magnesium and calcium ions (Mg^{2+} and Ca^{2+})
b Sodium carbonate
c Pass the water through an ion exchange column, this removes the Ca^{2+} and Mg^{2+} ions and replaces them with sodium or hydrogen ions
d It does not lather well, so more soap is used to get a lather and a scum forms
e The Ca^{2+} ions are good for our health (bones and teeth)

4 a Fats and oils, carbohydrates
b Your body stores the excess as fat
c Obesity

d

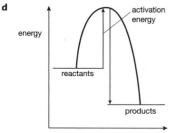

Ion present
Potassium K^+
Iron(III) Fe^{3+}
Copper(II) Cu^{2+}
Chloride Cl^-
Sulfate SO_4^{2-}
Carbonate CO_3^{2-} (a metal such as Mg or Zn would also be correct)

5

GCSE Physics

1 **a** The force is the gravitational force due to the Earth

  b 1 day (24 hours)

  c The satellite has a constant acceleration and a constant centripetal force; the direction of the centripetal force and the acceleration is towards the Earth's centre

  d They are used for communications

2 **a** The image in a plane mirror is always virtual, upright and the same height as the object

  b A converging lens has a real (principal) focus, whereas the diverging lens has a virtual focus

  c **i**

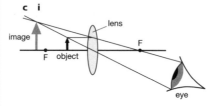

    ii The image is virtual and magnified